A BALANCED MATHEMATICS PROGRAM INTEGRATING SCIENCE AND LANGUAGE ARTS

Unit Resource Guide
Unit 17

Wholes
and Parts

THIRD EDITION

KENDALL/HUNT PUBLISHING COMPANY
4050 Westmark Drive   Dubuque, Iowa 52002

A TIMS® Curriculum
University of Illinois at Chicago

UIC The University of Illinois
at Chicago

The original edition was based on work supported by the National Science Foundation under grant No. MDR 9050226 and the University of Illinois at Chicago. Any opinions, findings, and conclusions or recommendations expressed in this publication are those of the author(s) and do not necessarily reflect the views of the granting agencies.

Letter Home

Wholes and Parts

Date: _____

Dear Family Member:

In this unit, *Wholes and Parts,* students will build on their understanding of fractions. They will participate in activities that develop several important fraction concepts.

One important idea is that fractional parts must be equal in size. Another is that you cannot know the size of a fraction unless you know the size of the whole: a half can be large or small depending on what it is half of. Half a pizza can be a lot or a little depending on the size of the pizza. A third important concept involves equivalent fractions. The same amount can be named in different ways: two-fourths, five-tenths, and one-half are all the same amount.

If students understand the basic concepts of fractions, they will be more proficient later when they calculate with them. You can help your child at home to explore fractions and practice math facts.

The Clever Tailor uses her fraction knowledge to win the day.

- **Cooking with Fractions.** When you cook with your child, ask what the whole is when you measure something. "If this is a third, what is the whole?" Ask if there is another name for a fraction in a recipe. "Is two-fourths cup of milk the same as half a cup?"

- **Everyday Fractions.** Talk with your child about fractions you encounter in everyday life. "If we live six blocks from school, how many blocks do we walk to get halfway there? Two-thirds of the way?"

- **Math Facts.** Help your child practice the multiplication facts for the threes and nines using the *Triangle Flash Cards.*

Thank you for helping your child learn and use mathematics.

Sincerely,

_____

Carta al hogar

Enteros y partes

Fecha: _____

Estimado miembro de familia:

En esta unidad, *Enteros y partes,* los estudiantes profundizarán su conocimiento sobre fracciones. Participarán en actividades que desarrollan varios conceptos importantes sobre fracciones.

Una idea importante es que las partes fraccionarias deben ser del mismo tamaño. Otra es que no se puede saber el tamaño de una fracción a menos que se sepa el tamaño del entero: una mitad puede ser grande o pequeña dependiendo de la mitad de qué cosa se trate. Media pizza puede ser mucho o poco dependiendo del tamaño de la pizza. Un tercer concepto importante tiene que ver con las fracciones equivalentes. La misma cantidad puede nombrarse de diferentes maneras: dos cuartos, cinco décimos y un medio son todas fracciones que representan el mismo número.

La sastrecilla inteligente usa su conocimiento de fracciones para salir ganando.

Si los estudiantes comprenden los conceptos básicos sobre fracciones, tendrán un mejor dominio de las fracciones cuando las usen para hacer cálculos en el futuro. Usted puede ayudar a su hijo/a a explorar las fracciones y practicar los conceptos matemáticos básicos en casa.

- **Cocinar con fracciones.** Cuando usted cocina con su hijo/a, pregúntele cuál es el entero cuando miden algo. "Si esto es un tercio, ¿cuánto es un entero?" Pregúntele si hay otra forma de llamar a alguna fracción de una receta. "¿Es dos cuartos de taza de leche lo mismo que media taza?"

- **Fracciones cotidianas.** Hable con su hijo/a acerca de las fracciones que se encuentran en la vida cotidiana. "Si vivimos a seis calles de la escuela, ¿cuántas calles debemos caminar para estar a mitad de camino? ¿Dos tercios del camino?"

- **Conceptos básicos.** Ayude a su hijo/a a practicar las tablas de multiplicación del tres y del nueve usando las tarjetas triangulares.

Gracias por ayudar a su hijo/a a aprender y usar las matemáticas.

Atentamente,

Table of Contents

Unit 17
Wholes and Parts

Unit 17

Outline
Wholes and Parts

Unit Summary

Estimated Class Sessions

6

Students explore relationships between fractions, focusing on the idea that fractional parts of a whole must have equal areas and on the concept of equivalence. The activities include the use of geoboards and paper folding. They also find that different fractions can represent the same quantity. They may even begin to notice patterns in those fractions. They are encouraged to think about relationships between fractions other than equivalence, including greater than, less than, and comparisons with benchmarks such as 0, 1, and $\frac{1}{2}$. In the Adventure Book, *The Clever Tailor,* misunderstandings about fractions arise when the size of the unit whole is ignored. The DPP for this unit provides practice with and assesses the multiplication facts for the threes and nines.

Major Concept Focus

- multiple representations of fractions
- fraction concepts
- concept of a whole
- area model of fractions
- part-whole fractions
- congruence
- flips
- one-half as a benchmark
- equivalent fractions
- comparing fractions
- *Adventure Book:* concept of a whole
- Game: comparing fractions
- patterns
- practice and assessment of the multiplication facts for the 3s and 9s

Pacing Suggestions

Lesson 3 *The Clever Tailor* is a story based on a fairy tale by the Brothers Grimm. Students can read the story as part of language arts.

Assessment Indicators

Use the following Assessment Indicators and the *Observational Assessment Record* that follows the Background section in this unit to assess students on key ideas.

A1. Can students represent fractions using geoboards and paper folding?

A2. Do students recognize that fractional parts of a whole must have equal areas but can have different shapes?

A3. Can students partition a shape into fractional parts?

A4. Can students find and name equivalent fractions using manipulatives?

A5. Do students demonstrate fluency with the multiplication facts for the 3s and 9s?

Unit Planner

	Lesson Information	Supplies	Copies/Transparencies
Lesson 1 **Geoboard Fractions** URG Pages 18–36 SG Pages 252–254 DPP A–D HP Parts 1–2 *Estimated Class Sessions* **2** 	**Activity** Students make rectangles on geoboards and find different ways to divide them into halves, thirds, and fourths. **Math Facts** DPP Bit A provides practice with multiplication facts for the threes and nines. **Homework** 1. Students use *Triangle Flash Cards* to study for the quiz on the threes and nines in DPP Bit K. 2. Assign Parts 1 and 2 of the Home Practice for homework. **Assessment** 1. Students complete the *Halves of a Rectangle* Assessment Blackline Masters. 2. Use the *Observational Assessment Record* to record students' abilities to partition shapes into fractional parts.	• 1 geoboard per student • overhead geoboard • several rubber bands per student	• 1 copy of *Halves of a Rectangle* URG Pages 28–29 per student • 2 copies of *Large Geoboard Paper* URG Page 30 per student • 4 copies of *Geoboard Paper* URG Page 31 per student • 1 copy of *Triangle Flash Cards:3s* and *9s* URG Pages 32–33 per student, optional • 1 transparency of *Large Geoboard Paper* URG Page 30 or overhead geoboard • 1 transparency of *Geoboard Paper* URG Page 31 • several copies of *Large Geoboard Paper* URG Page 30 • 1 copy of *Observational Assessment Record* URG Pages 9–10 to be used throughout this unit
Lesson 2 **Folding Fractions** URG Pages 37–51 SG Pages 255–263 DAB Pages 253–254 DPP E–H *Estimated Class Sessions* **2** 	**Activity** Students find equivalent forms for $\frac{1}{2}$, $\frac{1}{3}$, and other simple fractions by folding paper. **Homework** Have students complete the Folding One-fourth section in class or for homework. **Assessment** 1. Use *Questions 48–50* in the Folding One-fourth section as assessment. 2. Use the *Observational Assessment Record* to document students' abilities to find and name equivalent fractions using manipulatives.	• several sheets of scratch paper (large enough to be folded several times and preferably blank on one side) per student • markers or crayons • 1 ruler per student, optional	• 2 copies of *One-third Folding Sheet* URG Page 46 per student
Lesson 3 **The Clever Tailor** URG Pages 52–61 AB Pages 115–128 DPP I–J HP Part 3 *Estimated Class Sessions* **1** 	**Adventure Book** This story complements the unit's fraction activities by helping students to see the misunderstandings about fractions that can arise when the size of the unit whole is ignored. **Math Facts** Bit I provides practice with the multiplication facts. Task J provides practice with multiplication facts for the 3s and 9s with multiples of 10 and 100. **Homework** 1. Have students find the prices of items in newspaper ads or catalogs. Then have them list things they would buy if they had $4050. Direct students to come as close to the figure as they can without going over.	• 1 meterstick per student, optional • play money: ten-, hundred-, and thousand-dollar bills, optional • pattern blocks, optional • counters, optional	

	Lesson Information	Supplies	Copies/Transparencies
	2. Suggest that students read the story to someone at home and discuss the story's fraction misunderstandings. 3. Assign Part 3 of the Home Practice. It reviews fractional parts using area models.		
Lesson 4 **Fraction Hex** URG Pages 62–67 DAB Pages 255–257 DPP K–L HP Part 4 *Estimated Class Sessions* **1**	**Game** Students compare fractions in the game *Fraction Hex.* **Math Facts** DPP Bit K is a short quiz that assesses multiplication facts for the threes and nines. **Homework** 1. Students take home *Fraction Hex* to play with their families. 2. Assign Part 4 of the Home Practice. **Assessment** 1. DPP Bit K Multiplication Quiz: 3s and 9s assesses the multiplication facts in these groups. 2. Transfer appropriate documentation from the Unit 17 *Observational Assessment Record* to students' *Individual Assessment Record Sheets.*	• 2 same color centimeter cubes or other game marker per student • pattern blocks • 1 clear plastic spinner or paper clip and pencil per student	• 1 copy of *Individual Assessment Record Sheet* TIG Assessment section per student, previously copied for use throughout the year.

Connections

A current list of literature and software connections is available at *www.mathtrailblazers.com.* You can also find information on connections in the *Teacher Implementation Guide* Literature List and Software List sections.

Literature Connections
Suggested Titles
- The *Adventure Book* in this unit, *The Clever Tailor,* is based on "The Valiant Little Tailor," a fairy tale by the Brothers Grimm. Two collections that include this story are:
  - *The Complete Grimm's Fairy Tales.* Pantheon Books, New York, 1980. (Lesson 3)
  - Lang, Andrew. *Blue Fairy Book.* Dover Publications, New York, 1975. (Lesson 3)
- Silverstein, Shel. "Smart" from *Where the Sidewalk Ends.* HarperCollins, New York, 1994. (Lesson 3)

Software Connections
- *Fraction Attraction* develops understanding of fractions using fraction bars, pie charts, hundreds blocks, and other materials.
- *National Library of Virtual Manipulatives* website (http://matti.usu.edu) allows students to work with manipulatives including geoboards and fraction pieces.
- *Shape Up!* is a geometry program that contains five sets of shapes that students can manipulate and explore.
- *Tenth Planet: Representing Fractions* provides a conceptual introduction to fractions.

Teaching All Math Trailblazers Students

Math Trailblazers® lessons are designed for students with a wide range of abilities. The lessons are flexible and do not require significant adaptation for diverse learning styles or academic levels. However, when needed, lessons can be tailored to allow students to engage their abilities to the greatest extent possible while building knowledge and skills.

To assist you in meeting the needs of all students in your classroom, this section contains information about some of the features in the curriculum that allow all students access to mathematics. For additional information, see the Teaching the *Math Trailblazers* Student: Meeting Individual Needs section in the *Teacher Implementation Guide.*

Differentiation Opportunities in this Unit

Games

Use games to promote or extend understanding of math concepts and to practice skills with children who need more practice.

- Lesson 4 *Fraction Hex*

Journal Prompts

Journal prompts provide opportunities for students to explain and reflect on mathematical problems. They can help both students who need practice explaining their ideas and students who benefit from answering higher order questions. Students with various learning styles can express themselves using pictures, words, and sentences. Teachers can alter journal prompts to suit students' ability levels. The following lessons contain a journal prompt:

- Lesson 1 *Geoboard Fractions*
- Lesson 2 *Folding Fractions*
- Lesson 3 *The Clever Tailor*

DPP Challenges

DPP Challenges are items from the Daily Practice and Problems that usually take more than fifteen minutes to complete. These problems are more thought-provoking and can be used to stretch students' problem-solving skills. The following lesson has a DPP Challenge in it:

- DPP Challenge H from Lesson 2 *Folding Fractions*

Extensions

Use extensions to enrich lessons. Many extensions provide opportunities to further involve or challenge students of all abilities. Take a moment to review the extensions prior to beginning this unit. Some extensions may require additional preparation and planning. The following lesson contains extensions:

- Lesson 1 *Geoboard Fractions*

Background
Wholes and Parts

In this last third-grade fraction unit, students revisit concepts involving the unit whole, fractional parts, and equivalent fractions. Students also explore the relative size of fractions, focusing on the size of one-half and translating between various representations of fractions including real situations, concrete models, words, pictures, and symbols. As in previous units, the importance of the whole is stressed. You may want to refer to the Background sections of Unit 13 *Parts and Wholes* and Unit 15 *Decimal Investigations* for further discussion of these ideas.

In Lesson 1 *Geoboard Fractions* students make rectangles on geoboards and then divide the rectangles into fractional parts in different ways. The activity reinforces the concept that fractional parts must have equal areas. Lesson 1 uses an area model for fractions. Lesson 2 *Folding Fractions* is a series of paper-folding exercises that show how different fractions can name the same quantity. Again an area model is used.

The Adventure Book *The Clever Tailor* involves the unit whole. In the story, the hero outwits her adversaries primarily through her superior understanding of the importance of the whole in determining the size of fractions. In *The Clever Tailor,* length, area, and discrete fraction models all appear.

The game in Lesson 4 *Fraction Hex* requires students to compare two fractions. Some fractions are equivalent. In *Fraction Hex,* no fraction model is specified, but students can use pattern block hexagons to solve the problems.

Observational Assessment Record

(A1) Can students represent fractions using geoboards and paper folding?

(A2) Do students recognize that fractional parts of a whole must have equal areas but can have different shapes?

(A3) Can students partition a shape into fractional parts?

(A4) Can students find and name equivalent fractions using manipulatives?

(A5) Do students demonstrate fluency with the multiplication facts for the 3s and 9s?

(A6) _____

Name	A1	A2	A3	A4	A5	A6	Comments
1.							
2.							
3.							
4.							
5.							
6.							
7.							
8.							
9.							
10.							
11.							
12.							
13.							

Name	A1	A2	A3	A4	A5	A6	Comments
14.							
15.							
16.							
17.							
18.							
19.							
20.							
21.							
22.							
23.							
24.							
25.							
26.							
27.							
28.							
29.							
30.							
31.							
32.							

Unit 17

Daily Practice and Problems
Wholes and Parts

A DPP Menu for Unit 17

Two Daily Practice and Problems (DPP) items are included for each class session listed in the Unit Outline. A scope and sequence chart for the DPP is in the *Teacher Implementation Guide*.

Icons in the Teacher Notes column designate the subject matter of each DPP item. The first item in each class session is always a Bit and the second is either a Task or Challenge. Each item falls into one or more of the categories listed below. A menu of the DPP items for Unit 17 follows.

N Number Sense	Computation	Time	Geometry
B, D, F–H, J, L	C, E, G, J		

Math Facts	$ Money	Measurement	Data
A, I–K	C	E	

Practicing and Assessing the Multiplication Facts

In Unit 11, students began the systematic, strategies-based study of the multiplication facts. In Unit 17, students review and practice the multiplication facts for threes and nines. The *Triangle Flash Cards* for these groups were distributed in Units 12 and 14 in the *Discovery Assignment Book* immediately following the Home Practice. They can also be found in Lesson 1 of the *Unit Resource Guide*. In Unit 17, DPP items A, I, and J provide practice with multiplication facts for these groups. Bit K is the Multiplication Quiz: 3s and 9s.

For information on the distribution and study of the multiplication facts in Grade 3, see the DPP Guide for Units 3 and 11. For a detailed explanation of our approach to learning and assessing the math facts in Grade 3 see the *Grade 3 Facts Resource Guide* and for information for Grades K–5, see the TIMS Tutor: *Math Facts* in the *Teacher Implementation Guide.*

Daily Practice and Problems

Students may solve the items individually, in groups, or as a class. The items may also be assigned for homework. The DPPs are also available on the Teacher Resource CD.

Student Questions	Teacher Notes

A Facts: 3s and 9s

A. $5 \times 3 =$

B. $3 \times 7 =$

C. $5 \times 9 =$

D. $3 \times 0 =$

E. $7 \times 9 =$

F. $8 \times 3 =$

G. $3 \times 3 =$

H. $10 \times 9 =$

I. $9 \times 9 =$

J. $9 \times 2 =$

K. $1 \times 9 =$

L. $2 \times 3 =$

Explain your strategies for Questions E and F.

TIMS Bit $\boxed{\begin{smallmatrix} 5 \\ \times\, 7 \end{smallmatrix}}$

A. 15	B. 21
C. 45	D. 0
E. 63	F. 24
G. 9	H. 90
I. 81	J. 18
K. 9	L. 6

Discuss strategies students use to solve the facts, emphasizing those that are more efficient than others. For example, skip counting for 3×3 (3, 6, 9) may be efficient; however, skip counting for 7×9 is not. Alternatively, to solve 7×9, students might use $7 \times 10 = 70$ and then subtract 7 to get 63. Knowing one fact may help in solving another. For example, by doubling the answer to 4×3, one can quickly get the answer to 8×3. Students also may say, "I just know it." Recall is obviously an efficient strategy.

Tell students to take home the *Triangle Flash Cards: 3s and 9s* to study for the quiz in DPP Bit K. The flash cards for these groups were distributed in Units 12 and 14 in the *Discovery Assignment Book* following the Home Practice. Flash cards are also available in Lesson 1.

Student Questions	Teacher Notes

B Counting by 0.5s

Use your calculator to count by 0.5 starting at any number. Then try these:

1. Count by 0.5s from 0 to 4. Say the numbers.

2. Count by 0.5s from 8 to 12. Write down the numbers.

3. Count by 0.5s from 98 to 102. Say the numbers.

4. Choose your own starting and stopping places for counting by 0.5s. Write down the numbers.

TIMS Task

Remind students to use proper punctuation such as commas to separate the numbers in their list.

1. If your calculator has the constant feature, press: 0 + .5 = = = etc. The constant number (.5) and the constant operation (addition) is repeated each time = is pressed. 0, 0.5, 1, 1.5, 2, 2.5, 3, 3.5, 4; Students should say, "five-tenths, one, one and five-tenths, two, . . . "

2. Press: 8 + .5 = = = etc. 8, 8.5, 9, 9.5, 10, 10.5, 11, 11.5, 12

3. Press: 98 + .5 = = etc. 98, 98.5, 99, 99.5, 100, 100.5, 101, 101.5, 102

C Colored Pencils

Randy has five quarters and five dimes. He wants to buy a box of colored pencils that costs $1.89.

1. Does Randy have enough money?

2. If he has too little money, then how much more does he need? Or if he has enough, how much change will he get?

TIMS Bit

1. No, he only has $1.75.

2. He needs 14 cents more.

D **Close Enough**

1. Write down two fractions close to 1/2, but not equal to 1/2.

2. Write down two fractions close to 1, but not equal to 1.

3. Write down two fractions close to 0, but not equal to 0.

TIMS Task

Answers will vary.

1. $\frac{6}{10}, \frac{4}{7}, \frac{5}{8}, \frac{51}{100}$

2. $\frac{99}{100}, \frac{11}{12}, \frac{9}{10}, \frac{11}{10}, \frac{5}{4}, \frac{10}{9}$

3. $\frac{1}{10}, \frac{1}{50}, \frac{1}{100}$

 E **Volume**

A graduated cylinder contains 5 marbles, each with a volume of 3 cc, and enough water so that the water level reading is 95 cc. How much water is in the container?

TIMS Bit

Suggest that students draw a picture to help them solve the problem.

80 cc; 95 cc − 5 × 3 cc = 80 cc

 F **Base-Ten Shorthand**

Write a common and decimal fraction for each of the following. A flat is one whole and a skinny represents one-tenth.

1.

2.

3.

4.

TIMS Task

1. $\frac{9}{10}$, 0.9

2. $1\frac{5}{10}$, 1.5

3. $3\frac{3}{10}$, 3.3

4. $2\frac{1}{10}$, 2.1

Student Questions	Teacher Notes

 Addition and Subtraction Practice

TIMS Bit

Complete the following problems. Use pencil and paper or mental math to find the answers.

1. Predict which of the following problems will have the largest answer (sum or difference).

2. 6590
   − 765

3. 5411
   +2387

4. 2948
   +1798

5. 9345
   −1197

1. Discuss students' predictions and strategies for finding the largest answer before solving the problem.

2. 5825

3. 7798

4. 4746

5. 8148

H **Fraction, Decimal, Percent**

TIMS Challenge

Write (a) a common fraction, (b) a decimal fraction, and (c) a percent for the shaded part of each picture.

1.

2.

3.

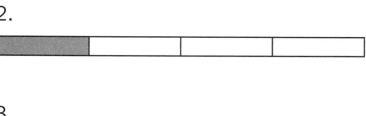

1. A. $\frac{5}{10}$ or $\frac{1}{2}$
   B. 0.5
   C. 50%

2. A. $\frac{1}{4}$
   B. 0.25
   C. 25%

3. A. $\frac{3}{4}$
   B. 0.75
   C. 75%

| Student Questions | Teacher Notes |

 Facts: 3s and 9s Again

TIMS Bit

A. 3	B. 27
C. 36	D. 24
E. 72	F. 21
G. 15	H. 12
I. 54	J. 30
K. 0	L. 18

A. $3 \times 1 =$ B. $3 \times 9 =$

C. $9 \times 4 =$ D. $8 \times 3 =$

E. $8 \times 9 =$ F. $3 \times 7 =$

G. $3 \times 5 =$ H. $4 \times 3 =$

I. $9 \times 6 =$ J. $10 \times 3 =$

K. $0 \times 9 =$ L. $3 \times 6 =$

Explain your strategies for Questions E and F.

Discuss strategies students use to solve the facts, emphasizing those that are more efficient than others. By subtracting 8 from the answer to 8×10 or 80, a student can quickly get the answer to 8×9. Knowing one fact may help in solving another. If a student knows $3 \times 6 = 18$, he or she can add 3 more to get the answer to 3×7.

Remind students to use the flash cards to study at home and tell them when you will give the quiz on these facts. The quiz is in DPP Bit K.

Multiples of 10 and 100

1. Solve the following problems.

   A. $3 \times 4 =$ B. $3 \times 40 =$

   C. $3 \times 400 =$ D. $400 \times 9 =$

   E. $300 \times 6 =$ F. $5 \times 60 =$

   G. $5 \times 59 =$ H. $4 \times 40 =$

   I. $4 \times 39 =$

2. Choose one of the problems. Draw a picture and write a story about it.

TIMS Task

The answer to Question F is 300. To do Question G, think: $5 \times 60 - 5 \times 1$. Discuss other strategies used to solve Questions 1G and 1I.

1. A. 12		B. 120	
C. 1200		D. 3600	
E. 1800		F. 300	
G. 295		H. 160	
I. 156			

2. Stories will vary.

Multiplication Quiz: 3s and 9s

Do these problems in your head. Write only the answers.

A. $3 \times 0 =$ B. $9 \times 4 =$

C. $9 \times 3 =$ D. $3 \times 7 =$

E. $0 \times 9 =$ F. $9 \times 8 =$

G. $4 \times 3 =$ H. $9 \times 2 =$

I. $9 \times 6 =$ J. $3 \times 8 =$

K. $3 \times 3 =$ L. $9 \times 5 =$

M. $9 \times 7 =$ N. $3 \times 2 =$

O. $6 \times 3 =$ P. $9 \times 9 =$

Q. $10 \times 3 =$ R. $5 \times 3 =$

S. $9 \times 10 =$ T. $9 \times 1 =$

TIMS Bit

We recommend 2 minutes for this quiz. Allow students to change pens or pencils after the time is up and complete the remaining problems in a different color. After students take the quiz, have them update their *Multiplication Facts I Know* charts.

A	0	B.	36
C.	27	D.	21
E.	0	F.	72
G.	12	H.	18
I.	54	J.	24
K.	9	L.	45
M.	63	N.	6
O.	18	P.	81
Q.	30	R.	15
S.	90	T.	9

 True or False?

Tell whether each number sentence is true or false. Explain how you know.

A. $1.4 > 5$

B. $0.9 > 1$

C. $1.4 = \frac{1}{4}$

D. $3.5 < 5.3$

TIMS Task Ⓝ

A. False; 1.4 means you have only 1 whole and some more but not 2 wholes.

B. False; 0.9 is less than 1 whole. It is like having 90 cents, not a whole dollar.

C. False; 1.4 is more than 1 whole. $\frac{1}{4}$ is only part of a whole.

D. True; 3.5 has only 3 wholes whereas 5.3 has 5 wholes.

Geoboard Fractions

Lesson Overview

Students divide geoboard rectangles into halves, thirds, and fourths in as many ways as possible. They record their divisions on *Geoboard Paper*.

Key Content

- Representing fractions using geoboards.
- Dividing a whole into equal-area parts.
- Measuring area by counting square units.
- Understanding that fractional parts of a whole must have equal areas but can have different shapes.
- Translating among different representations of fractions (concrete, pictorial, and symbolic).
- Identifying congruent shapes.

Key Vocabulary

- congruent

Math Facts

DPP Bit A provides practice with multiplication facts for the threes and nines.

Homework

1. Students use *Triangle Flash Cards* to study for the quiz on the threes and nines in DPP Bit K.
2. Assign Parts 1 and 2 of the Home Practice for homework.

Assessment

1. Students complete the *Halves of a Rectangle* Assessment Blackline Masters.
2. Use the *Observational Assessment Record* to record students' abilities to partition shapes into fractional parts.

Curriculum Sequence

Fractions

Students explored fractions in Grade 3 Unit 13 *Parts and Wholes* and Grade 3 Unit 15 *Decimal Investigations*. In Unit 13, they used pattern blocks to find the unit whole when given a fractional part and to find a fractional part when given the unit whole. In Unit 15, they explored decimal fractions.

Congruence, Flips, and Dissections

Students explored concepts of congruence, including flipping, in Grade 2 Unit 15 *Geometry in Motion*. They learned that two-dimensional shapes can be manipulated by flips, slides, and turns. In Grade 3 Unit 12 *Dissections* students solved problems using concepts of congruence. They manipulated shapes by flipping them to make designs with tangram pieces. They also solved dissection puzzles.

Fractions

Students will study fractions and decimals in increasing depth in Grades 4 and 5. See Grade 4 Units 10 and 12 and Grade 5 Units 3, 5, 7, 9, and 12.

Materials List

Supplies and Copies

Student	Teacher
Supplies for Each Student • geoboard • several rubber bands	**Supplies** • overhead geoboard
Copies • 1 copy of *Halves of a Rectangle* per student (*Unit Resource Guide* Pages 28–29) • 2 copies of *Large Geoboard Paper* per student (*Unit Resource Guide* Page 30) • 4 copies of *Geoboard Paper* per student (*Unit Resource Guide* Page 31) • 1 copy of *Triangle Flash Cards:3s* and *9s* per student, optional (*Unit Resource Guide* Pages 32–33)	**Copies/Transparencies** • 1 transparency of *Large Geoboard Paper* or overhead geoboard (*Unit Resource Guide* Page 30) • 1 transparency of *Geoboard Paper* (*Unit Resource Guide* Page 31) • several copies of *Large Geoboard Paper* (*Unit Resource Guide* Page 30) • 1 copy of *Observational Assessment Record* to be used throughout this unit (*Unit Resource Guide* Pages 9–10)

All blackline masters including assessment, transparency, and DPP masters are also on the Teacher Resource CD.

Student Books
Geoboard Fractions (*Student Guide* Pages 252–254)

Daily Practice and Problems and Home Practice
DPP items A–D (*Unit Resource Guide* Pages 12–14)
Home Practice Part 1–2 (*Discovery Assignment Book* Page 250)

Note: Classrooms whose pacing differs significantly from the suggested pacing of the units should use the Math Facts Calendar in Section 4 of the *Facts Resource Guide* to ensure students receive the complete math facts program.

Assessment Tools
Observational Assessment Record (*Unit Resource Guide* Pages 9–10)

Daily Practice and Problems

Suggestions for using the DPPs are on page 26.

A. Bit: Facts: 3s and 9s (URG p. 12)

A. $5 \times 3 =$ B. $3 \times 7 =$
C. $5 \times 9 =$ D. $3 \times 0 =$
E. $7 \times 9 =$ F. $8 \times 3 =$
G. $3 \times 3 =$ H. $10 \times 9 =$
I. $9 \times 9 =$ J. $9 \times 2 =$
K. $1 \times 9 =$ L. $2 \times 3 =$

Explain your strategies for Questions E and F.

B. Task: Counting by 0.5s (URG p. 13)

Use your calculator to count by 0.5 starting at any number. Then try these:

1. Count by 0.5s from 0 to 4. Say the numbers.
2. Count by 0.5s from 8 to 12. Write down the numbers.
3. Count by 0.5s from 98 to 102. Say the numbers.
4. Choose your own starting and stopping places for counting by 0.5s. Write down the numbers.

C. Bit: Colored Pencils (URG p. 13)

Randy has five quarters and five dimes. He wants to buy a box of colored pencils that costs $1.89.

1. Does Randy have enough money?
2. If he has too little money, then how much more does he need? Or if he has enough, how much change will he get?

D. Task: Close Enough (URG p. 14)

1. Write down two fractions close to 1/2, but not equal to 1/2.
2. Write down two fractions close to 1, but not equal to 1.
3. Write down two fractions close to 0, but not equal to 0.

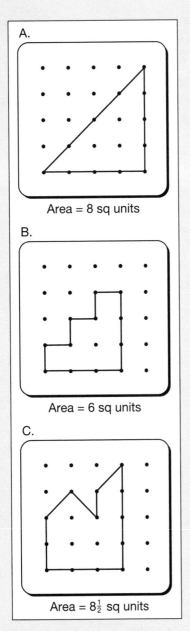

A.

Area = 8 sq units

B.

Area = 6 sq units

C.

Area = $8\frac{1}{2}$ sq units

Figure 1: *Students find the area of shapes like these to begin the lesson*

Teaching the Activity

The activities in *Geoboard Fractions* use an area model to emphasize two points about fractions: (1) The whole must be divided into equal-area parts, but (2) those parts do not have to be congruent. By learning these two points, students will understand part-whole fractions better.

The *Geoboard Fractions* Activity Pages consist of three parts: Making Halves, Making Thirds, and Making Fourths. Making Halves is described in detail below. The other two parts are similar and are described more briefly.

Part 1 Making Halves

Start this activity by reviewing with students how to find the area of a two-dimensional shape by counting interior units. Demonstrate with a few examples on the overhead geoboard or transparency of *Geoboard Paper* Blackline Master. Include a few irregular shapes that require counting half units to find the area. See Figure 1 for examples.

When students are comfortable with finding area, display a 2-unit by 4-unit rectangle on the overhead geoboard. Ask:

*   *What is the area of this shape?* (8 square units)
*   *What does it mean to divide this shape in half?* (Divide it into two parts of the same size or divide it "fairly.")
*   *Can someone come to the overhead and show how to divide this shape in half?*
*   *Explain why these two parts can be called "halves."* (Each part is the same size.)
*   *How do we know?* (Each has the same number of square units.)

Precisely what "equal" and "fair" mean can be put aside for the moment.

Using the first page of *Geoboard Fractions* in the *Student Guide* for guidance, have students copy the 2-by-4 rectangle on their geoboards using rubber bands and find as many ways as possible to divide it in half. As they find ways to halve the rectangle, ask them to keep records on their copies of the *Geoboard Paper* Blackline Master. Suggest they color each half with a different color and write fractions to identify how much each color represents (such as $\frac{1}{2}$ red, $\frac{1}{2}$ blue).

After students record their ways to halve the rectangle, use copies of *Large Geoboard Paper* Blackline Master to post examples on a wall or bulletin board so all students can see them. Several ways of dividing the rectangle into halves are shown in Figure 2. There are other ways that are not shown.

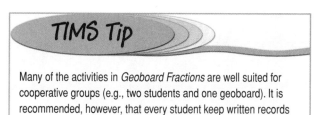

Many of the activities in *Geoboard Fractions* are well suited for cooperative groups (e.g., two students and one geoboard). It is recommended, however, that every student keep written records on his or her own *Geoboard Paper*.

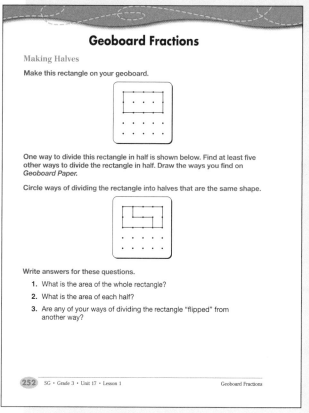

Student Guide - page 252 *(Answers on p. 34)*

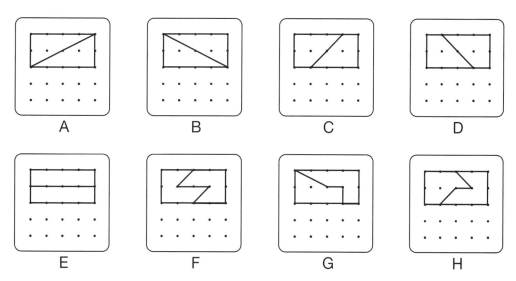

Figure 2: *Eight of the many ways to divide the rectangle into halves*

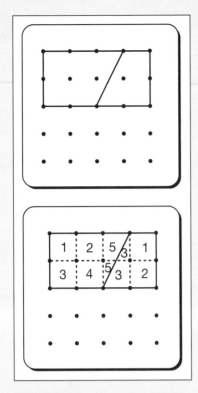

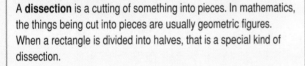

Figure 3: *Two parts that are not halves as shown by counting square units*

Content Note

A **dissection** is a cutting of something into pieces. In mathematics, the things being cut into pieces are usually geometric figures. When a rectangle is divided into halves, that is a special kind of dissection.

Journal Prompt

Imagine you have divided something into two parts. What must be true about the area of the parts for them to be halves? Draw an example in which the two parts are halves and an example in which the two parts are not halves.

Question 2 asks students what the area of each half is (4 square units since the whole rectangle has an area of 8 square units). If no student discovered them, model at least one of the irregular divisions shown in Figure 2 (C, D, F, G, H). Guide students to count the square units, including half-units, to find that the area of each of the two partitions is the same, 4 square units.

Some students might propose something like Figure 3 as a solution.

- *Why are these two pieces not halves?* (They do not have the same area.)

- *How can we make sure this is true?* (By counting square units.)

Question 3 asks students to identify flips. Ask students to find similarities between the examples of divided rectangles, called dissections. They might see that two dissections, such as Examples A and B in Figure 2, look much the same—Example B is Example A flipped over. Show this by drawing the figure on the overhead transparency and then flipping it over. Examples C and D are also "flips" of one another. At first glance, students may think that if the geoboard is turned (not flipped), they can get Example B from Example A. Let students try it to see that turning does not work for Examples A and B or Examples C and D. You can let the class decide whether they want to consider two solutions that are flips of one another different solutions or the same.

Another noticeable thing about these dissections is that, in many, the pieces are the same shape as well as the same size—they are **congruent.** Remind students of the definition of **congruence** from Unit 12: Two shapes are congruent if they have the same size and shape, so that you can turn or flip one to cover the other exactly. In Figure 2, Examples A, B, C, D, E, and F have congruent halves; Examples G and H have halves that are not congruent. Have students sort their own dissections into two groups, one with halves that are congruent, the other with halves that are not. Students can verify whether two halves are congruent by recording the dissection on a copy of *Large Geoboard Paper* Blackline Master, cutting the halves out, and checking whether they match when one is laid on the other.

Part 2 Making Thirds and Fourths

Use *Questions 4–5* to have students divide a 3-by-4 rectangle into thirds of equal area and record their solutions on *Geoboard Paper*. They will then shade the thirds that have the same shape (are congruent) and write a fraction for the amount shaded. Either no thirds, two thirds, or all three thirds should be shaded for each dissection. For *Questions 6–7,* students are to divide a 3-by-4 rectangle into fourths, record their solutions on *Geoboard Paper,* shade a number of fourths, and write a fraction to show the amount shaded.

Model one or two of the irregular partitions and guide the class in finding the areas by counting the square units. See Figure 4 for examples.

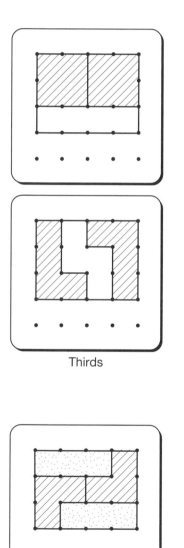

Thirds

Fourths

Figure 4: *Irregular partitions for thirds and fourths*

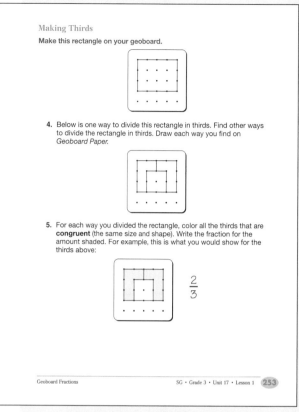

Student Guide - page 253 (Answers on p. 34)

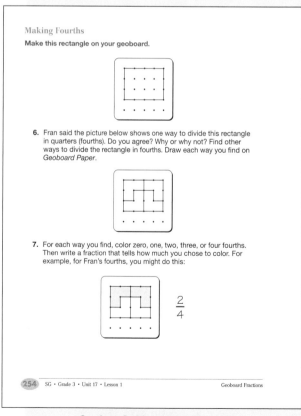

Student Guide - page 254 (Answers on p. 35)

DPP Bit A provides practice with the multiplication facts for the threes and nines.

- DPP Task B builds number sense for decimals by skip counting. Bit C provides word problems involving money. Task D builds number sense for fractions.

- Tell students to use the *Triangle Flash Cards: 3s* and *Triangle Flash Cards: 9s* to study at home for the quiz on these facts in DPP Bit K.

- Assign Parts 1 and 2 of the Home Practice for homework. These problems provide practice with estimation and computation with pencil and paper.

Answers for Parts 1 and 2 of the Home Practice are in the Answer Key at the end of this lesson and at the end of this unit.

- The *Halves of a Rectangle* Assessment Blackline Masters ask students to show ways to divide a rectangle in half, to identify dissections in which the halves are congruent, and to find the areas of the whole square and half the square.

- Use the *Observational Assessment Record* to note students' abilities to partition a shape into fractional parts.

Many extensions of this lesson are possible. Here are some questions for further investigation:

- How can all rectangles on a geoboard be divided in half using rubber bands?

- Can all rectangles be divided in thirds on the geoboard? If not, which ones can?

- How can all rectangles be divided in fourths on the geoboard? Find one way that will work for all rectangles.

At a Glance

Math Facts and Daily Practice and Problems

DPP Bit A provides practice with multiplication facts for the threes and nines. Tasks B and D build number sense. Bit C involves computations with money.

Teaching the Activity

1. Review finding area of geoboard shapes by counting square units.
2. Introduce the *Geoboard Fractions* Activity Pages in the *Student Guide* by displaying a 2-unit by 4-unit rectangle on the *Geoboard Paper* transparency.
3. Discuss what it means to divide a shape in half.
4. Students copy the 2-by-4 rectangle on their geoboards and find ways to divide it in half.
5. Students find the area of each half of the rectangle.
6. On *Geoboard Paper,* students record ways to divide the rectangle in half.
7. Use *Large Geoboard Paper* to post ways students divided the rectangle in half.
8. Model partitioning as shown in one or more of the examples shown in Figure 2.
9. Students look for similarities in the examples of dissections posted on *Large Geoboard Paper.*
10. Students sort their dissections into two groups, one with halves that are congruent, and one with halves that are not.
11. For *Questions 4–5,* students divide a 3-by-4 rectangle into thirds, record their solutions on *Geoboard Paper,* shade the thirds that are congruent, and write a fraction for the amount shaded.
12. For *Questions 6–7,* students divide a 3-by-4 rectangle into fourths, record their solutions on *Geoboard Paper,* shade a number of fourths, and write a fraction for the amount shaded.

Homework

1. Students use *Triangle Flash Cards* to study for the quiz on the threes and nines in DPP Bit K.
2. Assign Parts 1 and 2 of the Home Practice for homework.

Assessment

1. Students complete the *Halves of a Rectangle* Assessment Blackline Masters.
2. Use the *Observational Assessment Record* to record students' abilities to partition shapes into fractional parts.

Extension

Ask questions to further students' explorations:
- How can all rectangles be divided in half on the geoboard?
- Can all rectangles be divided in thirds on the geoboard?
- How can all rectangles be divided into fourths on the geoboard?

Answer Key is on pages 34–36.

Notes:

Halves of a Rectangle

Find different ways to divide in half the rectangles shown on the geoboards below. Did you find halves that are *congruent* (the same shape and size)? Did you find halves that are not congruent (different shapes)? Draw each way you find below. Circle the rectangles that have congruent halves.

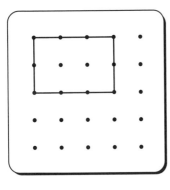 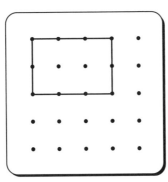 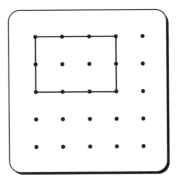

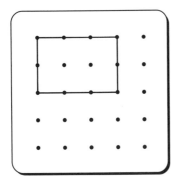 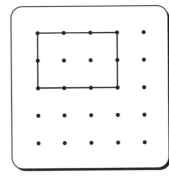 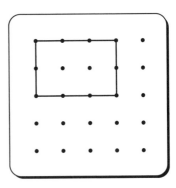

Answer these questions.

1. What is the area of the rectangle? _____

2. What is the area of each half? _____

Assessment Blackline Master

3. The square to the right is divided into halves. Tell how you know.

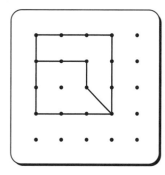

4. Are the halves congruent? Tell how you know.

Large Geoboard Paper

Geoboard Paper

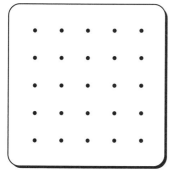
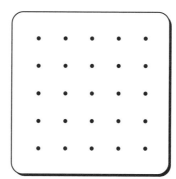
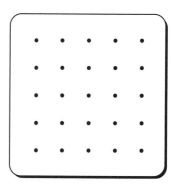

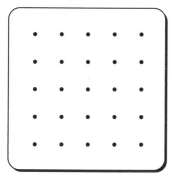
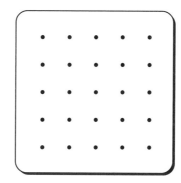
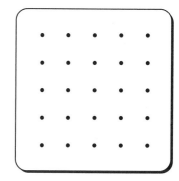

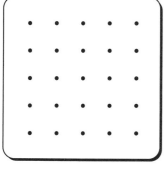
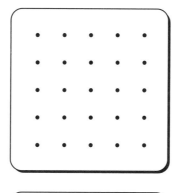
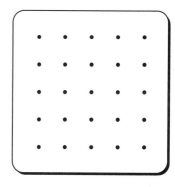

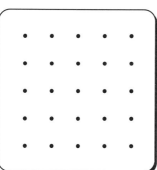
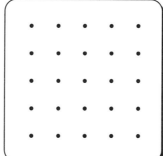
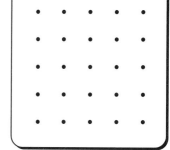

Triangle Flash Cards: 3s

- Work with a partner. Each partner cuts out the flash cards below.

- Your partner chooses one card at a time and covers the shaded corner.

- Multiply the two uncovered numbers.

- Divide the used cards into three piles: those you know and can answer quickly, those you can figure out, and those you need to learn.

- Practice the last two piles again. Then make a list of the facts you need to practice at home.

- Repeat the directions for your partner.

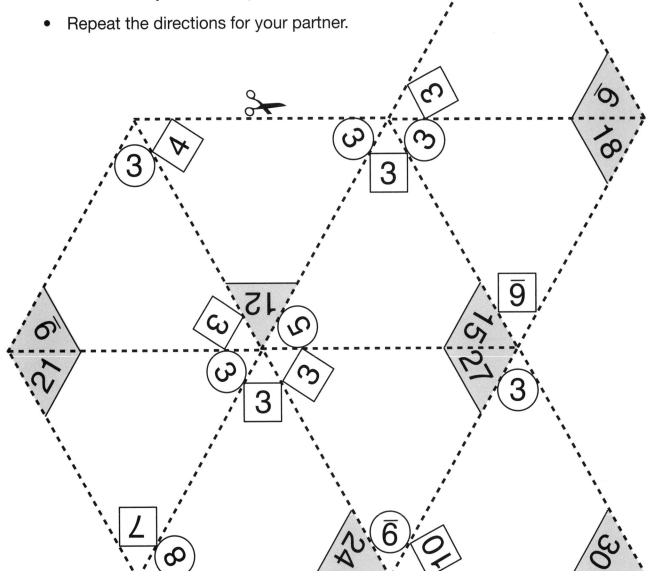

Blackline Master

Triangle Flash Cards: 9s

- Work with a partner. Each partner cuts out the 9 flash cards.

- Your partner chooses one card at a time and covers the shaded number.

- Multiply the two uncovered numbers.

- Divide the used cards into three piles: those you know and can answer quickly, those you can figure out, and those you need to learn.

- Practice the last two piles again. Then make a list of the facts you need to practice at home.

- Repeat the directions for your partner.

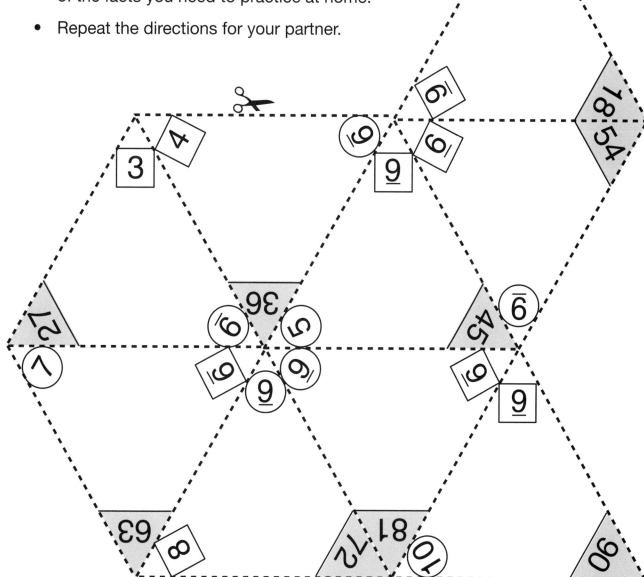

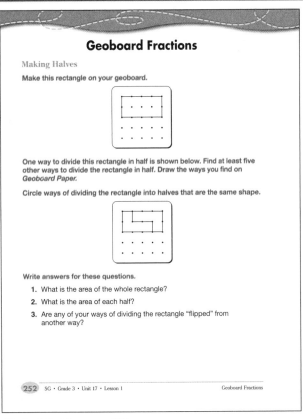

Student Guide - page 252

Student Guide (p. 252)

Geoboard Fractions*

1. 8 square units

2. 4 square units

3. Answers will vary.

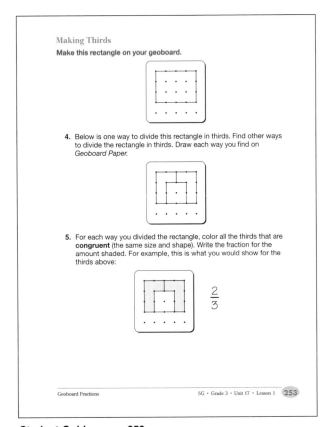

Student Guide - page 253

Student Guide (p. 253)

4. Answers will vary. Here are three examples:

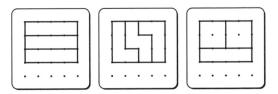

5. Answers will vary. Here are three examples:

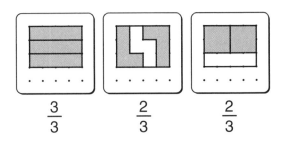

$$\frac{3}{3} \qquad \frac{2}{3} \qquad \frac{2}{3}$$

*Answers and/or discussion are included in the Lesson Guide.

Student Guide (p. 254)

6. Yes; each part has the same area—3 square units.
Answers will vary. Here are three examples:

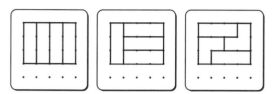

7. Answers will vary. Here are three examples:

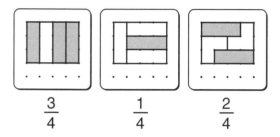

$$\frac{3}{4} \qquad \frac{1}{4} \qquad \frac{2}{4}$$

Discovery Assignment Book (p. 250)

Home Practice*

Part 1

1. 137
2. 145
3. 64
4. 67
5. **A.** 77 and 85
   B. 77 and 26
   C. 48 and 26
   D. 85 and 77

Part 2

1. 382
2. 570
3. 6642
4. 3589
5. Strategies will vary. Possible strategy:
   $470 + 4 + 96 =$
   $\qquad 470 + 100 = 570.$
6. **A.** more than 100 times
   B. $11.30

*Answers for all the Home Practice in the *Discovery Assignment Book* are at the end of the unit.

Making Fourths
Make this rectangle on your geoboard.

6. Fran said the picture below shows one way to divide this rectangle in quarters (fourths). Do you agree? Why or why not? Find other ways to divide the rectangle in fourths. Draw each way you find on Geoboard Paper.

7. For each way you find, color zero, one, two, three, or four fourths. Then write a fraction that tells how much you chose to color. For example, for Fran's fourths, you might do this:

$\frac{2}{4}$

254 SG • Grade 3 • Unit 17 • Lesson 1   Geoboard Fractions

Student Guide - page 254

Name _____ Date _____

Unit 17 **Home Practice**

PART 1
Use your estimating skills to help you solve the following problems.

| 1. 87 +50 | 2. 87 +58 | 3. 94 −30 | 4. 94 −27 |

5. Which two numbers below should you add if you want an answer:

   77   85   26   48

   A. over 150? _____
   B. very close to 100? _____
   Which two numbers should you subtract if you want an answer:
   C. close to 25? _____
   D. less than 10? _____

PART 2
| 1. 335 +47 | 2. 474 +96 | 3. 6931 −289 | 4. 7030 −3441 |

5. Explain a strategy for solving Question 2 using mental math.

6. In a jump-a-thon for heart disease, Linda jumped rope 42 times without tripping. Carol jumped 33 times. Michael jumped 38 times.
   A. Did this group jump more or less than 100 times? _____
   B. One sponsor agreed to pay the group of three 10¢ for each jump. How much money did they earn from the sponsor?

250 DAB • Grade 3 • Unit 17   WHOLES AND PARTS

Discovery Assignment Book - page 250

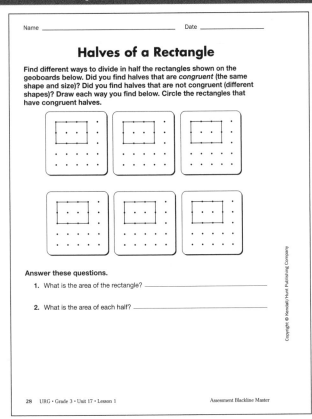

Name _____ Date _____

Halves of a Rectangle

Find different ways to divide in half the rectangles shown on the geoboards below. Did you find halves that are *congruent* (the same shape and size)? Did you find halves that are not congruent (different shapes)? Draw each way you find below. Circle the rectangles that have congruent halves.

Answer these questions.

1. What is the area of the rectangle? _____

2. What is the area of each half? _____

28   URG • Grade 3 • Unit 17 • Lesson 1   Assessment Blackline Master

Unit Resource Guide - page 28

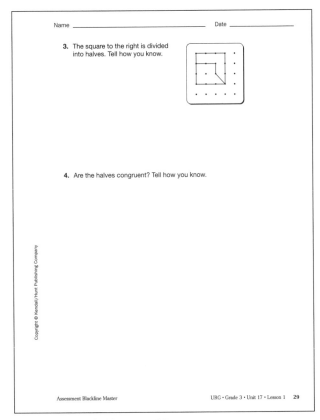

Name _____ Date _____

3. The square to the right is divided into halves. Tell how you know.

4. Are the halves congruent? Tell how you know.

Assessment Blackline Master   URG • Grade 3 • Unit 17 • Lesson 1   29

Unit Resource Guide - page 29

Unit Resource Guide (pp. 28–29)

Halves of a Rectangle

Answers will vary. Here are nine possibilities. All the rectangles have congruent halves.

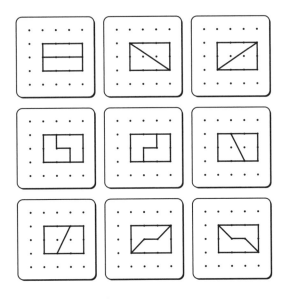

1. 6 square units

2. 3 square units

3. The areas are the same—$4\frac{1}{2}$ square units.

4. No, they are not congruent. They are not the same shape. One piece is shaped like an "L," the other is not.

Lesson 2

Folding Fractions

Lesson Overview

Estimated Class Sessions

2

Students fold and color sheets of scratch paper to find and to name fractions that are equivalent to one-half, one-third, and one-fourth. Children record in a table the data they generate from the paper-folding activities. Then they analyze the data to identify patterns in equivalent fractions.

Key Content

• Identifying equivalent fractions through paper-folding activities.

• Finding patterns in equivalent fractions.

Key Vocabulary

• equivalent

Homework

Have students complete the Folding One-fourth section in class or for homework.

Assessment

1. Use *Questions 48–50* in the Folding One-fourth section as assessment.
2. Use the *Observational Assessment Record* to document students' abilities to find and name equivalent fractions using manipulatives.

Materials List

Supplies and Copies

Student	Teacher
Supplies for Each Student • several sheets of scratch paper (large enough to be folded several times and preferably blank on one side) • markers or crayons • ruler, optional	**Supplies**
Copies • 2 copies of *One-third Folding Sheet* per student (*Unit Resource Guide* Page 46)	**Copies/Transparencies**

All blackline masters including assessment, transparency, and DPP masters are also on the Teacher Resource CD.

Student Books

Folding Fractions (*Student Guide* Pages 255–263)
Folding Fractions Data Tables (*Discovery Assignment Book* Pages 253–254)

Daily Practice and Problems and Home Practice

DPP items E–H (*Unit Resource Guide* Pages 14–15)

Note: Classrooms whose pacing differs significantly from the suggested pacing of the units should use the Math Facts Calendar in Section 4 of the *Facts Resource Guide* to ensure students receive the complete math facts program.

Assessment Tools

Observational Assessment Record (*Unit Resource Guide* Pages 9–10)

E. Bit: Volume (URG p. 14)

A graduated cylinder contains 5 marbles, each with a volume of 3 cc, and enough water so that the water level reading is 95 cc. How much water is in the container?

G. Bit: Addition and Subtraction Practice (URG p. 15)

Complete the following problems. Use pencil and paper or mental math to find the answers.

1. Predict which of the following problems will have the largest answer (sum or difference).

2. $\begin{array}{r} 6590 \\ -\ 765 \\ \hline \end{array}$ 3. $\begin{array}{r} 5411 \\ +2387 \\ \hline \end{array}$

4. $\begin{array}{r} 2948 \\ +1798 \\ \hline \end{array}$ 5. $\begin{array}{r} 9345 \\ -1197 \\ \hline \end{array}$

F. Task: Base-Ten Shorthand (URG p. 14)

Write a common and decimal fraction for each of the following. A flat is one whole and a skinny represents one-tenth.

1. |/\|||||
2. ||/||▢
3. ||▢|▢▢
4. ▢|/\||||/|||

H. Challenge: Fraction, Decimal, Percent (URG p. 15)

Write (a) a common fraction, (b) a decimal fraction, and (c) a percent for the shaded part of each picture.

1.
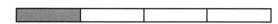

2.

3.

Student Guide - page 255

Folding Fractions

Folding One-third

We have many ways to name the same number. For example, we can name the number 5 by writing 1 + 4 or 2 + 3. We can also name 700 + 80 + 3 by writing the number 783. A lot of the work of arithmetic is finding other names for numbers.

We have different names for fractions, too. Another name for one-third is two-sixths. When two fractions name the same number, we say they are **equivalent**. The word *equivalent* means equal or equal value. So we can say that one-third is equivalent to two-sixths.

In this activity, you will find and name fractions that are equivalent to one-third. Follow these steps.

1. Use the *One-third Folding Sheet*. Fold it on the lines into three equal parts.

2. Unfold the paper. Then color one of the thirds.

3. Use the One-third data table in your *Discovery Assignment Book*. It is like the one below. Fill in the first row as shown below.

One-third

Colored Parts	Total Parts	Fraction Colored
1	3	$\frac{1}{3}$

Student Guide - page 255 (Answers on p. 47)

Student Guide - page 256

4. Now, fold the paper in half the other way as shown in the picture below. Unfold the paper and trace the folds.

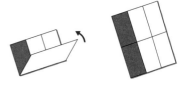

5. Count the colored parts, and count all the parts. Write these numbers in the first two columns of the One-third data table. Then in the last column, write a fraction that is equivalent to one-third.

6. Fold the paper as you did in Question 4. Then fold it in half the long way. Look at the picture below.

7. How many total parts do you think the paper will have when you unfold it?

8. Unfold the paper and trace the folds. Then count the colored parts and the total parts. Use your paper to find another fraction that is equivalent to one-third. Fill in the third row in the One-third data table.

Now you need to get another One-third Folding Sheet.

9. Fold the new sheet of paper in thirds the long way, as you did in Question 1. Then unfold it and color one of the thirds.

Student Guide - page 256 (Answers on p. 47)

Teaching the Activity

Launch the activity by discussing the concept of equivalence with students. Draw a pizza on the board and divide into thirds, explaining that three girls are going to share it equally.

See Figure 5. Ask:

- *How much pizza will each girl get?* (1/3)

Divide the pizza into sixths and ask:

- *If I divide the pizza into sixths, how much pizza will each girl get?* (2/6)

Divide the pizza into twelfths and ask:

- *If I divide the pizza into twelfths, how much pizza will each girl get?* (4/12)

- *Did each girl get more pizza when it was divided into thirds than when it was divided into sixths? (No) into twelfths?* (No)

- *Which way of dividing gave each girl more pizza? (None, their shares were the same with all ways of dividing.)*

Point out that whether each girl got $\frac{1}{3}$, $\frac{2}{6}$ or $\frac{4}{12}$ of the pizza, each got the same amount of pizza each time as shown in Figure 5.

Alternatively, you can use overhead pattern blocks to review equivalent fractions. If the yellow hexagon is one whole, then one blue ($\frac{1}{3}$) can be covered by two greens ($\frac{1}{6} + \frac{1}{6}$), showing that $\frac{1}{3}$ is equivalent to $\frac{2}{6}$. Discuss the first two paragraphs on the *Folding Fractions* Activity Pages in the *Student Guide*.

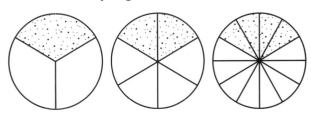

Figure 5: *Sharing a pizza to show that $\frac{2}{6}$ and $\frac{4}{12}$ are each equivalent to $\frac{1}{3}$*

After introducing equivalent fractions, explain to students that they will do paper-folding activities to find fractions that are equivalent to one-third, one-half, and one-fourth. We recommend that you work through

TIMS Tip

Students may use scratch paper to complete the folding activities. However, make sure they do not use paper that has been folded previously. Old letters may have been folded into thirds and the folds may confuse students.

the Folding One-third section on the *Folding Fractions* Activity Pages in the *Student Guide* with the students. These pages guide students in the proper paper-folding procedures for finding fractions equivalent to one-third. Each student needs two copies of the *One-third Folding Sheet* Blackline Master to complete this part of the activity. This sheet helps students fold a piece of paper into thirds by providing guidelines for where the folds should be. Students will also need the *Folding Fractions Data Tables* in the *Discovery Assignment Book* to record their work. As students create fractions equivalent to $\frac{1}{3}$ by folding paper, they complete a data table as shown in Figure 6.

One-third

Colored Parts	Total Parts	Fraction Colored
1	3	$\frac{1}{3}$
2	6	$\frac{2}{6}$
4	12	$\frac{4}{12}$
3	9	$\frac{3}{9}$
6	18	$\frac{6}{18}$

Figure 6: *A completed table for Folding One-third*

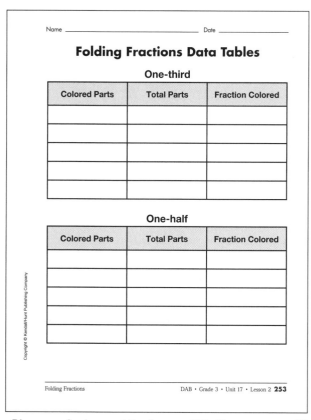

10. Fold the paper into thirds the other way. Then unfold the paper and trace the folds.

11. Count the parts and fill in another row in the One-third data table.

12. Fold the paper as you did in Question 10. Then fold it in half the long way. Look at the picture below.

13. How many total parts do you think the paper will have when you unfold it?

14. Unfold the paper and trace the folds. Then count the parts and fill in another row in the One-third data table.

15. The table should now have five rows filled in. What patterns do you notice?

16. A. Is $\frac{5}{15}$ equivalent to $\frac{1}{3}$? Why or why not?
    B. Find other fractions that are equivalent to one-third.

17. How do you know if a fraction is equivalent to one-third?

Student Guide - page 257 *(Answers on p. 47)*

Name _____ Date _____

Folding Fractions Data Tables

One-third

Colored Parts	Total Parts	Fraction Colored

One-half

Colored Parts	Total Parts	Fraction Colored

Discovery Assignment Book - page 253 *(Answers on p. 50)*

Name _____ Date _____

One-fourth

Colored Parts	Total Parts	Fraction Colored

Discovery Assignment Book - page 254 *(Answers on p. 51)*

In **Question 1** students fold their *One-third Folding Sheet* into thirds the long way or lengthwise along the lines. In **Question 10,** however, students are asked to fold it into thirds "the other way." Ask them to look at the picture that follows **Question 10.** Demonstrate the fold.

Question 15 in the Folding One-third section of the lesson asks students to notice patterns in the table. Possible patterns include:

- The total number of parts is always three times the number of colored parts;

- Three is a factor of all the numbers in the "Total Parts" column;

- The denominator is always three times the numerator.

Folding One-half

This activity is like *Folding One-third* except that you will find fractions that are equivalent to one-half. You will need several sheets of paper.

18. Get a sheet of paper. Fold the paper in half the long way. Be sure the two parts are the same size.

19. Unfold the paper, and draw a line between the halves. Then color one of the halves.

20. Use the One-half data table in your *Discovery Assignment Book*, similar to the one below. Fill in the first row as shown below.

One-half

Colored Parts	Total Parts	Fraction Colored
1	2	$\frac{1}{2}$

21. Now fold the paper in half the other way.

Student Guide - page 258 *(Answers on p. 48)*

---

22. Unfold the paper and trace the fold. Count the colored parts and count all the parts. Write the numbers in the first two columns of the One-half data table. Then, in the last column, write a fraction that is equivalent to one-half.

23. Fold the paper as you did in Question 21. Then fold it in half the long way. Look at the picture below.

24. How many total parts do you think there will be when you unfold the paper?

25. Unfold the paper and trace the folds. Then count the colored parts and the total parts. Use your paper to find another fraction that is equivalent to one-half. Fill in the third row in the One-half data table.

Now you need to get another piece of paper.

26. Fold your new piece of paper in half the long way. Unfold it. Draw a line between the halves. Then color one of the halves.

27. Fold the paper into three equal parts the other way. Then unfold the paper and trace the folds.

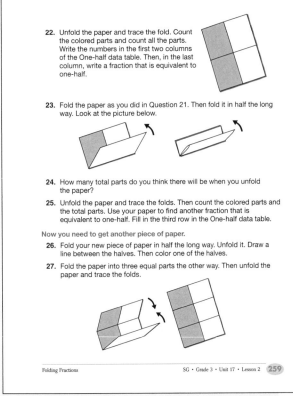

Student Guide - page 259 *(Answers on p. 48)*

---

28. Count the parts and fill in another row in the One-half data table.

29. Fold the paper into thirds as you did in Question 27. Then fold it in half the long way. Look at the picture below.

30. How many total parts do you think the paper will have when you unfold it?

31. Unfold the paper and trace the folds. Then count the parts, and fill in another row in the One-half data table.

32. The table should now have five rows filled in. What patterns do you notice?

33. Find other fractions that are equivalent to one-half.

34. How do you know if a fraction is equivalent to one-half?

Folding One-fourth

You have folded and colored paper to find fractions that are equivalent to one-half and one-third. Now you will fold and color paper to find fractions that are equivalent to one-fourth. You will need at least two pieces of paper.

35. Fold a sheet of paper the long way into four equal parts. To do this, fold the paper in half the long way. Then fold it in half the long way again.

Student Guide - page 260 *(Answers on p. 48)*

The students can use these patterns to answer **Questions 16** and **17**. We know that $\frac{5}{15}$ is equivalent to $\frac{1}{3}$ since the denominator (15) is 3 times the numerator (5). The important idea to stress is that each of the different fractions in the third column of the data table covers the same amount of area on the paper— each covers $\frac{1}{3}$ of the paper. **Questions 16** and **17** require students to generalize this concept.

Depending on the amount of success students experienced with Folding One-third, you can have them work through the section Folding One-half **(Questions 18–34)** independently, in groups, or as a class. These *Student Guide* pages guide the children in the proper paper-folding procedures for finding fractions equivalent to one-half, recording their work in a data table, and finding patterns in the equivalent fractions.

Journal Prompt

Tell about a time when you shared something and got a fraction of the whole. Find another fraction that is equivalent to the share you got.

---

36. Use the One-fourth data table in your *Discovery Assignment Book*. Fill in the first row as shown below. This fraction should describe the sheet of paper that you folded and colored in Question 35.

One-fourth

Colored Parts	Total Parts	Fraction Colored
1	4	$\frac{1}{4}$

37. Now fold the paper in half the other way as in the picture below. Unfold the paper and trace the folds.

38. Count the colored parts and then count all the parts. Write the numbers in the first two columns of the table. Then, in the last column, write a fraction that is equivalent to one-fourth.

39. Fold the paper as you did in Question 37. Then fold it again as shown in the picture below.

Student Guide - page 261 *(Answers on p. 49)*

---

40. How many total parts do you think the paper will have when you unfold it?

41. Unfold the paper and trace the folds. Then count the colored parts and the total parts. Use your paper to find another fraction that is equivalent to one-fourth. Fill in the third row in the table.

Now you need to get another sheet of paper.

42. Fold the new sheet of paper in fourths the long way as you did in Question 35. Unfold it and trace the lines between the fourths. Then color one of the fourths.

43. Fold the paper into thirds the other way as shown in the picture. Then unfold it, and trace the folds.

44. Fill in another row in the table.

45. Fold the paper as you did in Question 43. Then fold it again as shown in the picture below.

46. How many total parts do you think the paper will have when you unfold it?

47. Unfold the paper and trace the folds. Then count the parts, and fill in another row in the table.

Student Guide - page 262 *(Answers on p. 49)*

---

48. The table should now have five rows filled in. What patterns do you notice?

49. Find another fraction equivalent to one-fourth. (Hint: You can write a fraction with 20 in the denominator.)

50. How do you know if a fraction is equivalent to one-fourth?

Student Guide - page 263 *(Answers on p. 50)*

Homework and Practice

- The Folding One-fourth section in the *Student Guide* leads students to finding fractions that are equivalent to one-fourth. Students may complete the Folding One-fourth section for homework. Students will need the One-fourth data table in the *Discovery Assignment Book.*

- For DPP Bit E students use computation to find the volume of water in a graduated cylinder. Task F asks students to translate between base-ten shorthand and decimal numbers. Bit G provides practice with paper-and-pencil computation. For Challenge H students interpret area models and write fractions, decimals, and percents.

Assessment

- Once students complete the One-fourth data table, you can use *Questions 48–50* to assess students' abilities to recognize and communicate patterns they see in the table and to find a fraction equivalent to another fraction.

- Use the *Observational Assessment Record* to note students' abilities to find and name equivalent fractions using paper folding.

At a Glance

Math Facts and Daily Practice and Problems

DPP Bits E and G provide computation practice. Items F and H provide practice with fractions, decimals, and percents.

Teaching the Activity

1. Discuss **equivalent** fractions. Draw three pizzas on the board. Divide one into thirds, one into sixths, and one into twelfths. Discuss the fraction of each pizza three students would get if they shared the pizza equally ($\frac{1}{3} = \frac{2}{6} = \frac{4}{12}$).
2. Work through the section Folding One-third on the *Folding Fractions* Activity Pages in the *Student Guide* with students. Each student needs two copies of the *One-third Folding Sheet* Blackline Master to complete this part of the activity.
3. Students record their work in the One-third data table in the *Discovery Assignment Book*.
4. Students look for patterns in the equivalent fractions in their tables and use the patterns to identify and write more equivalent fractions in *Questions 15–17*.
5. Students work through the section Folding One-half independently, in groups, or as a class.

Homework

Have students complete the Folding One-fourth section in class or for homework.

Assessment

1. Use *Questions 48–50* in the Folding One-fourth section as assessment.
2. Use the *Observational Assessment Record* to document students' abilities to find and name equivalent fractions using manipulatives.

Answer Key is on pages 47–51.

Notes:

Name _____ Date _____

One-third Folding Sheet

Student Guide (pp. 255–257)

Folding Fractions

See Figure 6 in the Lesson Guide for a completed One-third data table.*

5. $\frac{2}{6}$

7. 12 parts

8. $\frac{4}{12}$

11. $\frac{3}{9}$

13. 18 parts

14. $\frac{6}{18}$

15. Answers will vary. Numbers in the Total Parts column are 3 times the numbers in the Colored Parts column. The colored parts are $\frac{1}{3}$ of the total parts. All the fractions in the Fraction Colored column have a denominator that is 3 times the numerator.*

16. A. Yes, because the denominator is three times larger than the numerator.*

B. Answers will vary. $\frac{7}{21}, \frac{8}{24}, \frac{10}{30}, \frac{20}{60}, \frac{50}{150}, \frac{100}{300}$, etc.

17. Answers will vary. The denominator will be three times larger than the numerator.*

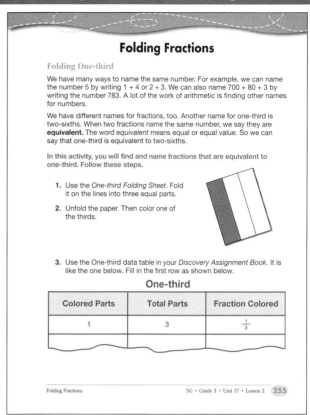

Student Guide - page 255

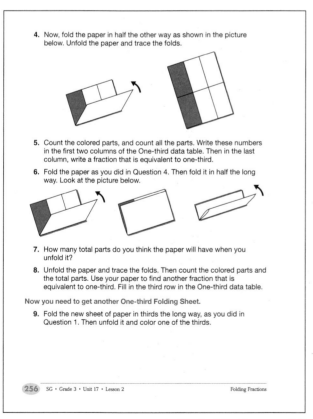

Student Guide - page 256

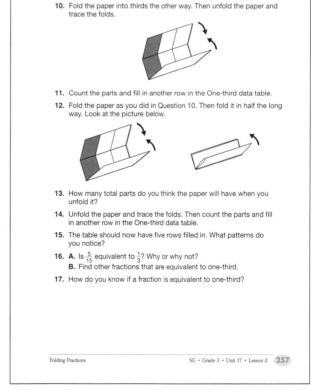

Student Guide - page 257

*Answers and/or discussion are included in the Lesson Guide.

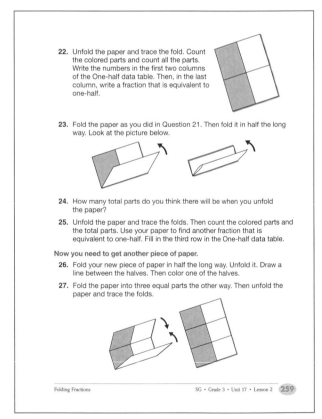

Student Guide - page 258

Student Guide (pp. 258–260)

See the *Discovery Assignment Book* Lesson 2 Answer Key for a completed One-half data table.

22. $\frac{2}{4}$

24. 8 parts

25. $\frac{4}{8}$

28. $\frac{3}{6}$

30. 12 parts

31. $\frac{6}{12}$

32. Answers will vary. The numbers in the Total Parts column are double the numbers in the Colored Parts column. The colored parts are $\frac{1}{2}$ of the total parts. All the fractions in the Fraction Colored column have denominators that are two times the numerator and equivalent to $\frac{1}{2}$.

33. Answers will vary. $\frac{5}{10}, \frac{7}{14}, \frac{8}{16}, \frac{10}{20}, \frac{15}{30}, \frac{20}{40}, \frac{50}{100}$, etc.

34. Answers will vary. The denominator is two times as large as the numerator.

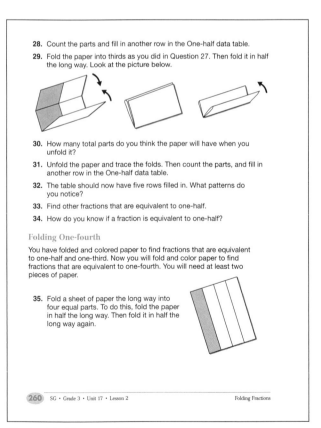

Student Guide - page 259

Student Guide - page 260

Student Guide (p. 261)

See the *Discovery Assignment Book* Lesson 2
Answer Key for a completed One-fourth data table.

38. $\frac{2}{8}$

---

36. Use the One-fourth data table in your *Discovery Assignment Book.* Fill in the first row as shown below. This fraction should describe the sheet of paper that you folded and colored in Question 35.

One-fourth

Colored Parts	Total Parts	Fraction Colored
1	4	$\frac{1}{4}$

37. Now fold the paper in half the other way as in the picture below. Unfold the paper and trace the folds.

38. Count the colored parts and then count all the parts. Write the numbers in the first two columns of the table. Then, in the last column, write a fraction that is equivalent to one-fourth.

39. Fold the paper as you did in Question 37. Then fold it again as shown in the picture below.

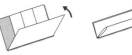

Student Guide - page 261

Student Guide (p. 262)

40. 16 parts

41. $\frac{4}{16}$

44. $\frac{3}{12}$

46. 24 parts

47. $\frac{6}{24}$

---

40. How many total parts do you think the paper will have when you unfold it?

41. Unfold the paper and trace the folds. Then count the colored parts and the total parts. Use your paper to find another fraction that is equivalent to one-fourth. Fill in the third row in the table.

Now you need to get another sheet of paper.

42. Fold the new sheet of paper in fourths the long way as you did in Question 35. Unfold it and trace the lines between the fourths. Then color one of the fourths.

43. Fold the paper into thirds the other way as shown in the picture. Then unfold it, and trace the folds.

44. Fill in another row in the table.

45. Fold the paper as you did in Question 43. Then fold it again as shown in the picture below.

46. How many total parts do you think the paper will have when you unfold it?

47. Unfold the paper and trace the folds. Then count the parts, and fill in another row in the table.

Student Guide - page 262

48. The table should now have five rows filled in. What patterns do you notice?

49. Find another fraction equivalent to one-fourth. (Hint: You can write a fraction with 20 in the denominator.)

50. How do you know if a fraction is equivalent to one-fourth?

Student Guide - page 263

Student Guide (p. 263)

48. Answers will vary. The numbers in the Total Parts column are 4 times the numbers in the Colored Parts column. The colored parts are $\frac{1}{4}$ of the total parts. All the fractions in the Fraction Colored column have denominators that are 4 times the numerators and are equivalent to $\frac{1}{4}$.

49. Answers will vary. $\frac{5}{20}, \frac{10}{40}, \frac{20}{80}, \frac{50}{200}, \frac{100}{400}$

50. Answers will vary. The denominator is 4 times as large as the numerator.

Name _____ Date _____

Folding Fractions Data Tables

One-third

Colored Parts	Total Parts	Fraction Colored

One-half

Colored Parts	Total Parts	Fraction Colored

Discovery Assignment Book - page 253

Discovery Assignment Book (p. 253)

Folding Fractions Data Tables

See Figure 6 in the Lesson Guide for a completed One-third data table.*

One-half

Colored Parts	Total Parts	Fraction Colored
1	2	$\frac{1}{2}$
2	4	$\frac{2}{4}$
4	8	$\frac{4}{8}$
3	6	$\frac{3}{6}$
6	12	$\frac{6}{12}$

*Answers and/or discussion are included in the Lesson Guide.

Discovery Assignment Book (p. 254)

One-fourth

Colored Parts	Total Parts	Fraction Colored
1	4	$\frac{1}{4}$
2	8	$\frac{2}{8}$
4	16	$\frac{4}{16}$
3	12	$\frac{3}{12}$
6	24	$\frac{6}{24}$

Name _____ Date _____

One-fourth

Colored Parts	Total Parts	Fraction Colored

254 DAB • Grade 3 • Unit 17 • Lesson 2   Folding Fractions

Discovery Assignment Book - page 254

Lesson 3

The Clever Tailor

Lesson Overview

This story complements the unit's fraction activities. A clever tailor sets off to seek her fortune and uses her knowledge of fractions to win against a giant and a band of robbers. She also helps three brothers divide their inheritance equally. Much of the action depends on misunderstandings about fractions that arise when the size of the unit whole is ignored.

The story's plot and several details are based on "The Valiant Little Tailor" by the Brothers Grimm.

Key Content

- Identifying the unit whole when a fraction is given.
- Understanding that fractional parts are equal.
- Finding a fractional part of a set.

Key Vocabulary

There is no key mathematical vocabulary. The following words from the story, however, may be unfamiliar to your students:

- disguise
- puny
- sash

Math Facts

Bit I provides practice with the multiplication facts. Task J provides practice with multiplication facts 3s and 9s with multiples of 10 and 100.

Homework

1. Have students find the prices of items in newspaper ads or catalogs. Then have them list things they would buy if they had $4050. Direct students to come as close to the figure as they can without going over.
2. Suggest that students read the story to someone at home and discuss the story's fraction misunderstandings.
3. Assign Part 3 of the Home Practice. It reviews fractional parts using area models.

Materials List

Supplies and Copies

Student	Teacher
Supplies for Each Student	**Supplies**
• meterstick, optional • play money: ten-, hundred-, and thousand-dollar bills, optional • pattern blocks, optional • counters, optional	
Copies	**Copies/Transparencies**

All blackline masters including assessment, transparency, and DPP masters are also on the Teacher Resource CD.

Student Books
The Clever Tailor (Adventure Book Pages 115–128)

Daily Practice and Problems and Home Practice
DPP items I–J (*Unit Resource Guide* Page 16)
Home Practice Part 3 (*Discovery Assignment Book* Page 251)

Note: Classrooms whose pacing differs significantly from the suggested pacing of the units should use the Math Facts Calendar in Section 4 of the *Facts Resource Guide* to ensure students receive the complete math facts program.

Daily Practice and Problems

Suggestions for using the DPPs are on page 60.

I. Bit: Facts: 3s and 9s Again (URG p. 16)

A. $3 \times 1 =$ B. $3 \times 9 =$
C. $9 \times 4 =$ D. $8 \times 3 =$
E. $8 \times 9 =$ F. $3 \times 7 =$
G. $3 \times 5 =$ H. $4 \times 3 =$
I. $9 \times 6 =$ J. $10 \times 3 =$
K. $0 \times 9 =$ L. $3 \times 6 =$

Explain your strategies for Questions E and F.

J. Task: Multiples of 10 and 100 (URG p. 16)

1. Solve the following problems.
   A. $3 \times 4 =$ B. $3 \times 40 =$
   C. $3 \times 400 =$ D. $400 \times 9 =$
   E. $300 \times 6 =$ F. $5 \times 60 =$
   G. $5 \times 59 =$ H. $4 \times 40 =$
   I $4 \times 39 =$

2. Choose one of the problems. Draw a picture and write a story about it.

Before the Adventure Book

In order to understand much of the story's action, students must understand the fallacy in thinking, for example, that two-thirds a slice of bread is more than one-half a loaf of bread. Some children might be fooled if they neglect to consider the whole for each fraction. Others might be confused by the relative size of the fractions. Address these issues before reading the story. Remind students to consider the whole for each fraction. Have students identify the larger number in each of the following pairs and explain their thinking using pattern blocks or drawings.

- $\frac{1}{2}$ and $\frac{2}{3}$
- $\frac{3}{4}$ and $\frac{9}{10}$
- $\frac{9}{10}$ and 1
- $\frac{1}{2}$ and $\frac{1}{4}$

Some of the fractions cannot easily be shown with pattern blocks, e.g., $\frac{9}{10}$. Show these fractions with a meterstick. Mark each fraction on the meterstick with tape, then use the meterstick as a length model for students. Fractions such as $\frac{2}{3}$ are not easy to show with precision on a meterstick, but students can estimate their size and relation to other fractions with the meterstick.

Discussion Prompts

The discussion prompts highlight much of the mathematics in the story. The first time you read the story, read it in its entirety without stopping for discussion. Then, reread it more slowly, drawing out the mathematics.

Page 117

- *What is three-fourths of four?*
Three.

- *What is three-fourths of 8?*
Six.

Repeat the question, substituting other numbers that can be manipulated evenly, such as 12 and 20. Students can use drawings or counters to solve the problems.

One fly got away, but she killed three.

"Oh, ho!" cried the tailor. "I have killed three-fourths of these flies with one blow! I am so strong! Three-fourths at one blow! What a hero I am!"

"Why should I be a tailor anymore? I will go into the world and seek my fortune," declared the tailor. "But first, I will make a sash so everyone will know who I am. I will sew 'Three-fourths at One Blow!' on the sash. Then, people will respect and fear me."

The Clever Tailor

AB • Grade 3 • Unit 17 • Lesson 3   117

Adventure Book - page 117

Page 118

- *What might the giant think "Three-fourths at One Blow!" means?*

It could mean that the tailor killed three-fourths of a group of *people* at one blow.

The Clever Tailor

So, the tailor made a sash with the words "Three-fourths at One Blow!" on it. She looked around her little room one last time and picked up her meterstick.

"This may be useful," she said.

She also took a piece of bread and her whistle. Then, our brave little tailor went forth into the world to seek her fortune.

She had not gone far when she met a huge and ugly giant.

"Who are you, little girl?" cried the giant in a voice like thunder. Then, he saw the sash. "Three-fourths at One Blow!" read the giant.

118   AB • Grade 3 • Unit 17 • Lesson 3

Adventure Book - page 118

Page 119

- *Is half a loaf of bread a lot to take in one bite?*

Yes, it's more than most people can bite!

The Clever Tailor

"You must be a great fighter. Come, maybe we can be friends."

But the tailor said, "I don't think I can be friendly with such a weak and puny man. Be careful with me, for I have killed three-fourths with one blow."

But the giant did not think he was weak and puny.

"Look, you," he said. "I can eat half of this loaf of bread in one bite. No little person can do that."

AB • Grade 3 • Unit 17 • Lesson 3   119

Adventure Book - page 119

The Clever Tailor

"That is nothing. Anybody can eat half in one bite," said the tailor. "Watch what someone who has killed three-fourths with one blow can do. Watch me eat two-thirds of this slice of bread in one bite."

Then, the tailor ate two-thirds of her slice of bread in one bite. And the giant was afraid.

Next, the giant said, "Look how high I can jump. I can jump three-fourths as high as that tree."

He showed her. But again, the tailor did not care.

Adventure Book - **page 120**

The Clever Tailor

"Look, you," said the tailor. "Show me something good or I will be angry. Watch how high I can jump. I can jump nine-tenths as high as this meterstick."

Then, the tailor did jump nine-tenths as high as her meterstick. And the giant was even more afraid.

"Watch out! Don't you try to hurt me," cried the giant. "I have ten brothers. If I blow this horn, nine-tenths of them will come at once. They will make you sorry."

"What? You dare to threaten one who has killed three-fourths with one blow?" asked the tailor. "I will blow my whistle, and **all** my sisters will come. Then, I think I will not be the one who is sorry."

Now, the tailor had no sisters, but the giant didn't know that. So, he was very afraid.

Adventure Book - **page 121**

Page 120

- *Which is bigger, one-half of something or two-thirds of the <u>same</u> thing?*

Two-thirds is bigger than one-half of the same thing. Compare drawings of $\frac{1}{2}$ and $\frac{2}{3}$ of the same size pizza or $\frac{1}{2}$ and $\frac{2}{3}$ of a yellow pattern block.

- *Is two-thirds a slice of bread a lot to take in one bite? Which is bigger, half a loaf or two-thirds a slice?*

Two-thirds a slice is not nearly as much as half a loaf of bread.

- *Give another example where half of something is bigger than two-thirds of something else.*

- *Is "three-fourths as high as a tree" a big jump?*

Yes, it's a very big jump.

- *How high is three-fourths of our classroom wall?* (Substitute any suitable object.)

Page 121

- *Which is bigger, nine-tenths of something or three-fourths of the <u>same</u> thing?*

Nine-tenths is bigger.

- *Show how high nine-tenths of a meterstick is. Show how high three-fourths of a meterstick is.*

- *Which is higher, nine-tenths of a meterstick or three-fourths of a tree?*

Three-fourths of a tall tree is considerably higher.

- *Give another example where nine-tenths of something is less than three-fourths of something else.*

- *How many is nine-tenths of ten brothers?*

Nine brothers.

- How many is all *of no sisters?*

None.

Page 122

- *How much is one-half of $100?*

$50.

- *How much is nine-tenths of $100?*

$90.

Adventure Book - page 122

Page 123

- *If the younger brothers each get one-fourth and the oldest brother gets one-half, each brother gets one piece. Is this a fair division?*

No, a fair division with three equal pieces means that each gets one-third.

Adventure Book - page 123

The Clever Tailor

"Our land is a rectangle that is 600 meters wide and 300 meters long," explained the middle brother as he drew a picture in the dirt with a stick.

"Now, my older brother wants to divide it like this," he continued, "but my younger brother and I don't think that's fair."

"I don't think it's fair either," said the tailor.

"But each of us gets one piece," said the oldest brother. "What could be more fair than that?"

"I think you need to make the pieces the same size," said the tailor. "Like this." The tailor drew this picture in the dirt.

"Now that's fair!" cried the two younger brothers.

The oldest brother had to agree. The three brothers were so happy to stop arguing that they gave the tailor $10.

"Thank you very much," said the brave little tailor. "Now, I must be on my way."

124   AB • Grade 3 • Unit 17 • Lesson 3

Adventure Book - page 124

The Clever Tailor

But some of the other robbers could read. They noticed the tailor's sash.

"What does that mean?" one robber asked. "Three-fourths at One Blow! Does that mean you can kill three-fourths of us with one blow?"

"How many of us is three-fourths?" asked another robber.

"Would you like to find out?" asked the tailor angrily. "I can show you right now if you want."

"No! No! Don't do that!" cried the robbers. "Calm down. We mean no harm."

"Well, that's better," said the tailor. "I mean no harm either, but you look poor. Do you need money?"

"We dress in these clothes to disguise ourselves," answered the robbers' leader. "Really, we are rich. We each have $1000 with us right now."

126   AB • Grade 3 • Unit 17 • Lesson 3

Adventure Book - page 126

Discussion Prompts

Page 124

- *How much money does the tailor have now?*

The tailor got $90 from the giant and $10 from the brothers, totaling $100.

Page 126

- *How many is three-fourths of eight robbers?*

Six.

- *How much money does each robber have?*

$1000.

- *How much money do the eight robbers have altogether?*

$1000 times eight robbers is $8000.

Page 127

• *Is the tailor's plan for sharing the money fair?*

No, she has less money at this point.

• *How much is half of the robbers' money?*

$4000.

• *How much is half of the tailor's money?*

$50.

• *Explain how the tailor ended up with $4050.*

The robbers give her half of their $8000—$4000. She gives them half of her $100—$50. So, each side now has $4050.

Adventure Book - page 127

Page 128

• *Who is that fancy lady?*

The tailor!

• *What is one-eighth of fifty?*

$6.25.

• *Who has more money now, the robbers or the tailor? Is this a coincidence?*

The robbers have the same amount as the tailor. They have the same amount because they got an equal share—half—of the two amounts. When the robbers divide up the money, however, each individual robber will get less.

The last frame may lead some students to conclude that the robbers have only $50. This is not true since they also have their original half of the $8000. The point of the story is that the robbers traded half of their money ($4000) and received only $50 in return. The $50 now has to be divided among the eight robbers to see what each got from the trade.

Adventure Book - page 128

Journal Prompt

Explain how the tailor used mathematics to trick the giant and the robbers.

Discovery Assignment Book - page 251 *(Answers on p. 61)*

Math Facts

DPP Bit I provides practice with the multiplication facts for the threes and nines. Task J also provides practice with these facts using multiples of 10 and 100.

Homework and Practice

- Have students find the prices of items in newspaper ads or catalogs. Then have them make a list of things they would buy if they had $4050. Direct students to come as close to this figure as they can without going over.

- Suggest students read the story to someone at home and discuss the story's fraction misunderstandings.

- Assign Part 3 of the Home Practice. It reviews fractional parts using area models.

Answers for Part 3 of the Home Practice are in the Answer Key at the end of this lesson and at the end of this unit.

Literature Connections

- *The Clever Tailor* is based on the fairy tale "The Valiant Little Tailor" by the Brothers Grimm. We suggest using either of the following two collections that include this story:

  1. *The Complete Grimm's Fairy Tales.* James Stern, ed. Pantheon Books, New York, 1980.

  2. *Lang, Andrew. Blue Fairy Book.* Dover Publications, New York, 1975.

- Silverstein, Shel. "Smart" from *Where the Sidewalk Ends*. HarperCollins, New York, 1994.

The narrator in the poem "Smart" has the same misunderstanding as the giant and the robbers in the Adventure Book. The narrator thinks that a greater number of coins means more money, not realizing it's the value of the coins that counts.

Discovery Assignment Book (p. 251)

Home Practice*

Part 3

1. **A.** $\frac{4}{10}$ or $\frac{2}{5}$
   B. $\frac{2}{5}$
   C. $\frac{4}{8}$ or $\frac{1}{2}$

2. **A.** less than
   B. less than
   C. equal to

3. 9 sq cm

4. $4\frac{1}{2}$ sq cm

Name _____ Date _____

PART 3

Use these pictures to answer Questions 1 and 2.

A.
B.
C.

1. What fraction of each rectangle above is shaded?
   A. _____ B. _____ C. _____

2. Are the shaded parts of each rectangle more than 50%, less than 50%, or equal to 50% of the whole rectangle?
   A. _____ B. _____ C. _____

Use this picture to answer Questions 3 and 4.

3. Area of the large square = _____

4. Area of shaded triangle = _____

PART 4

1. If this is 1 cubic centimeter: [ ], what is the volume of A and B?
   A. _____ B. _____

2. Draw 18 squares on a separate piece of paper (or use grid paper).
   A. Color 1/2 of the 18 squares red.
   B. Color 1/3 of the 18 squares blue.
   C. Color 1/6 of the 18 squares green.

WHOLES AND PARTS   DAB • Grade 3 • Unit 17 **251**

Copyright © Kendall/Hunt Publishing Company

Discovery Assignment Book - page 251

*Answers for all the Home Practice in the *Discovery Assignment Book* are at the end of the unit.

Lesson 4

Fraction Hex

Lesson Overview

Estimated Class Sessions

1

Students move two tokens to travel across a game board by correctly comparing the size of two fractions.

Key Content

- Comparing and ordering fractions.

Math Facts

DPP Bit K is a short quiz that assesses multiplication facts for the threes and nines.

Homework

1. Students take home *Fraction Hex* to play with their families.
2. Assign Part 4 of the Home Practice.

Assessment

1. DPP Bit K Multiplication Quiz: 3s and 9s assesses the multiplication facts in these groups.
2. Transfer appropriate documentation from the Unit 17 *Observational Assessment Record* to students' *Individual Assessment Record Sheets*.

Curriculum Sequence

In Units 12 and 15, students were introduced to the games *Hex* and *Decimal Hex,* which are versions of the game in this lesson.

Materials List

Supplies and Copies

Student	Teacher
Supplies for Each Student • 2 same color centimeter cubes or other game marker • pattern blocks • clear plastic spinner or paper clip and pencil	**Supplies**
Copies	**Copies/Transparencies**

All blackline masters including assessment, transparency, and DPP masters are also on the Teacher Resource CD.

Student Books
Fraction Hex (*Discovery Assignment Book* Pages 255–257)

Daily Practice and Problems and Home Practice
DPP items K–L (*Unit Resource Guide* Page 17)
Home Practice Part 4 (*Discovery Assignment Book* Page 251)

Note: Classrooms whose pacing differs significantly from the suggested pacing of the units should use the Math Facts Calendar in Section 4 of the *Facts Resource Guide* to ensure students receive the complete math facts program.

Assessment Tools
Observational Assessment Record (*Unit Resource Guide* Pages 9–10)
Individual Assessment Record Sheet (*Teacher Implementation Guide,* Assessment section)

K. Bit: Multiplication Quiz: 3s and 9s

(URG p. 17)

Do these problems in your head. Write only the answers.

A. $3 \times 0 =$	B. $9 \times 4 =$
C. $9 \times 3 =$	D. $3 \times 7 =$
E. $0 \times 9 =$	F. $9 \times 8 =$
G. $4 \times 3 =$	H. $9 \times 2 =$
I. $9 \times 6 =$	J. $3 \times 8 =$
K. $3 \times 3 =$	L. $9 \times 5 =$
M. $9 \times 7 =$	N. $3 \times 2 =$
O. $6 \times 3 =$	P. $9 \times 9 =$
Q. $10 \times 3 =$	R. $5 \times 3 =$
S. $9 \times 10 =$	T. $9 \times 1 =$

L. Task: True or False? (URG p. 17)

Tell whether each number sentence is true or false. Explain how you know.

A. $1.4 > 5$

B. $0.9 > 1$

C. $1.4 = \frac{1}{4}$

D. $3.5 < 5.3$

Name _____ Date _____

Fraction Hex

Players

This is a game for two or three players.

Materials

- *Fraction Hex Game Board*
- two same color centimeter cubes or other markers for each player
- one clear plastic spinner or pencil and paper clip

Fraction Hex

Discovery Assignment Book - page 255

Teaching the Game

Each player places two same color centimeter cubes or other game markers on two matching hexagons with the same number. The goal is to get the two cubes to the matching hexagons on the opposite side of the board. To move, a player spins the spinner. If the spinner shows greater than or equal to, the player can move either of the cubes to an adjacent hexagon with a fraction that is greater than or equal to his or her current position. If the spinner shows less than or equal to, the player moves one cube to an adjacent hexagon with a fraction that is less than or equal to his or her current position. The *Fraction Hex* Game Pages in the *Discovery Assignment Book* present the rules in detail. Students can model the fractions with pattern blocks that are shown on the Game Pages in the *Discovery Assignment Book* and use the pieces to make comparisons.

Name _____ Date _____

Rules

The goal of this game is to move two cubes or other game markers from matching hexagons to opposite matching hexagons that have the same number.

1. Each player places both of his or her cubes on two matching hexagons on one side of the game board. The target hexagons are the matching ones on the other side of the game board.

2. The first player spins the spinner.

3. If "Greater Than or Equal To" shows, the player may move one cube to a neighboring hexagon with a number that is greater than or equal to the number in the hexagon where the cube is now.

4. If "Less Than or Equal To" shows, the player may move one cube to a neighboring hexagon with a number that is less than or equal to the number in the hexagon where the cube is now.

5. The player may not be able to move a cube during his or her turn.

6. More than one cube can be on the same hexagon at the same time.

7. Players take turns spinning the spinner and moving cubes.

8. The first player to get **both** cubes to his or her target hexagons is the winner.

256 DAB • Grade 3 • Unit 17 • Lesson 4   Fraction Hex

Discovery Assignment Book - page 256

Name _____ Date _____

Use pattern blocks or these pictures to compare fractions.

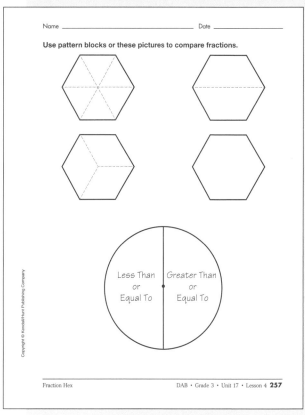

Fraction Hex   DAB • Grade 3 • Unit 17 • Lesson 4 **257**

Discovery Assignment Book - page 257

Homework and Practice

- Students take home *Fraction Hex* to play with their families. They will need their *Fraction Hex* Game Pages in the *Discovery Assignment Book.*

- For DPP Task L students compare fractions and decimals.

- You can assign Part 4 of the Home Practice for homework. It reviews volume and fractional parts of a set.

Answers for Part 4 of the Home Practice are in the Answer Key at the end of this lesson and at the end of this unit.

Assessment

- DPP Bit K is Multiplication Quiz: 3s and 9s. It assesses the multiplication facts in these groups.

- Transfer appropriate documentation from the Unit 17 *Observational Assessment Record* to students' *Individual Assessment Record Sheets.*

Name _____ Date _____

PART 3

Use these pictures to answer Questions 1 and 2.

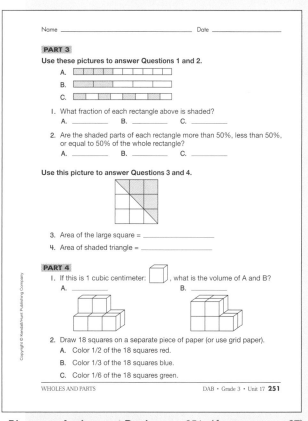

1. What fraction of each rectangle above is shaded?
   A. _____   B. _____   C. _____

2. Are the shaded parts of each rectangle more than 50%, less than 50%, or equal to 50% of the whole rectangle?
   A. _____   B. _____   C. _____

Use this picture to answer Questions 3 and 4.

3. Area of the large square = _____

4. Area of shaded triangle = _____

PART 4

1. If this is 1 cubic centimeter: [cube], what is the volume of A and B?
   A. _____   B. _____

2. Draw 18 squares on a separate piece of paper (or use grid paper).
   A. Color 1/2 of the 18 squares red.
   B. Color 1/3 of the 18 squares blue.
   C. Color 1/6 of the 18 squares green.

WHOLES AND PARTS   DAB • Grade 3 • Unit 17 **251**

Discovery Assignment Book - page 251 (Answers on p. 67)

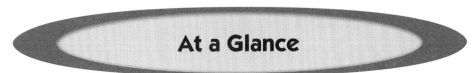

At a Glance

Math Facts and Daily Practice and Problems

DPP Bit K is a short quiz that assesses multiplication facts for the threes and nines. Task L involves comparing fractions and decimals.

Teaching the Game

1. Students read the rules on the *Fraction Hex* Game Pages in the *Discovery Assignment Book.*
2. Students play *Fraction Hex.*

Homework

1. Students take home *Fraction Hex* to play with their families.
2. Assign Part 4 of the Home Practice.

Assessment

1. DPP Bit K Multiplication Quiz: 3s and 9s assesses the multiplication facts in these groups.
2. Transfer appropriate documentation from the Unit 17 *Observational Assessment Record* to students' *Individual Assessment Record Sheets.*

Answer Key is on page 67.

Notes:

Discovery Assignment Book (p. 251)

Home Practice*

Part 4

1. **A.** 8 cubic centimeters

   B. 10 cubic centimeters

2. **A.** 9 squares will be red

   B. 6 squares will be blue

   C. 3 squares will be green

Name _____ Date _____

PART 3

Use these pictures to answer Questions 1 and 2.

A. ▭▭▭▭▭▭▭▭
B. ▭▭▭▭▭▭
C. ▭▭▭▭▭▭

1. What fraction of each rectangle above is shaded?
   A. _____ B. _____ C. _____

2. Are the shaded parts of each rectangle more than 50%, less than 50%, or equal to 50% of the whole rectangle?
   A. _____ B. _____ C. _____

Use this picture to answer Questions 3 and 4.

3. Area of the large square = _____

4. Area of shaded triangle = _____

PART 4

1. If this is 1 cubic centimeter: ▢ , what is the volume of A and B?
   A. _____ B. _____

2. Draw 18 squares on a separate piece of paper (or use grid paper).
   A. Color 1/2 of the 18 squares red.
   B. Color 1/3 of the 18 squares blue.
   C. Color 1/6 of the 18 squares green.

WHOLES AND PARTS   DAB • Grade 3 • Unit 17 **251**

Copyright © Kendall/Hunt Publishing Company

Discovery Assignment Book - page 251

---

*Answers for all the Home Practice in the *Discovery Assignment Book* are at the end of the unit.

Discovery Assignment Book (p. 250)

Part 1

1. 137
2. 145
3. 64
4. 67
5. **A.** 77 and 85
   B. 77 and 26
   C. 48 and 26
   D. 85 and 77

Part 2

1. 382
2. 570
3. 6642
4. 3589
5. Strategies will vary. Possible strategy:
   $470 + 4 + 96 =$
   $470 + 100 = 570.$
6. **A.** more than 100 times
   B. $11.30

Discovery Assignment Book (p. 251)

Part 3

1. **A.** $\frac{4}{10}$ or $\frac{2}{5}$
   B. $\frac{2}{5}$
   C. $\frac{4}{8}$ or $\frac{1}{2}$
2. **A.** less than
   B. less than
   C. equal to
3. 9 sq cm
4. $4\frac{1}{2}$ sq cm

Part 4

1. **A.** 8 cubic centimeters
   B. 10 cubic centimeters
2. **A.** 9 squares will be red
   B. 6 squares will be blue
   C. 3 squares will be green

Discovery Assignment Book - page 250

Discovery Assignment Book - page 251

Glossary

This glossary provides definitions of key vocabulary terms in the Grade 3 lessons. Locations of key vocabulary terms in the curriculum are included with each definition. Components Key: URG = *Unit Resource Guide,* SG = *Student Guide,* and DAB = *Discovery Assignment Book.*

A

Area (URG Unit 5; SG Unit 5)
The area of a shape is the amount of space it covers, measured in square units.

Array (URG Unit 7 & Unit 11)
An array is an arrangement of elements into a rectangular pattern of (horizontal) rows and (vertical) columns. (*See* column and row.)

Associative Property of Addition (URG Unit 2)
For any three numbers $a, b,$ and c we have $a + (b + c) = (a + b) + c$. For example in finding the sum of 4, 8, and 2, one can compute $4 + 8$ first and then add 2: $(4 + 8) + 2 = 14$. Alternatively, we can compute $8 + 2$ and then add the result to 4: $4 + (8 + 2) = 4 + 10 = 14$.

Average (URG Unit 5)
A number that can be used to represent a typical value in a set of data. (*See also* mean and median.)

Axes (URG Unit 8; SG Unit 8)
Reference lines on a graph. In the Cartesian coordinate system, the axes are two perpendicular lines that meet at the origin. The singular of axes is axis.

B

Base (of a cube model) (URG Unit 18; SG Unit 18)
The part of a cube model that sits on the "ground."

Base-Ten Board (URG Unit 4)
A tool to help children organize base-ten pieces when they are representing numbers.

Base-Ten Pieces (URG Unit 4; SG Unit 4)
A set of manipulatives used to model our number system as shown in the figure at the right. Note that a skinny is made of 10 bits, a flat is made of 100 bits, and a pack is made of 1000 bits.

Base-Ten Shorthand (SG Unit 4)
A pictorial representation of the base-ten pieces as shown.

Nickname	Picture	Shorthand
bit		•
skinny		/
flat		
pack		

Best-Fit Line (URG Unit 9; SG Unit 9; DAB Unit 9)
The line that comes closest to the most number of points on a point graph.

Bit (URG Unit 4; SG Unit 4)
A cube that measures 1 cm on each edge. It is the smallest of the base-ten pieces that is often used to represent 1.
(*See also* base-ten pieces.)

C

Capacity (URG Unit 16)
1. The volume of the inside of a container.
2. The largest volume a container can hold.

Cartesian Coordinate System (URG Unit 8)
A method of locating points on a flat surface by means of numbers. This method is named after its originator, René Descartes. (*See also* coordinates.)

Centimeter (cm)
A unit of measure in the metric system equal to one-hundredth of a meter. (1 inch = 2.54 cm)

Column (URG Unit 11)
In an array, the objects lined up vertically.

Common Fraction (URG Unit 15)
Any fraction that is written with a numerator and denominator that are whole numbers. For example, $\frac{3}{4}$ and $\frac{9}{4}$ are both common fractions. (*See also* decimal fraction.)

Commutative Property of Addition (URG Unit 2 & Unit 11)
This is also known as the Order Property of Addition. Changing the order of the addends does not change the sum. For example, $3 + 5 = 5 + 3 = 8$. Using variables, $n + m = m + n$.

Commutative Property of Multiplication (URG Unit 11)
Changing the order of the factors in a multiplication problem does not change the result, e.g., $7 \times 3 = 3 \times 7 = 21$. (*See also* turn-around facts.)

Congruent (URG Unit 12 & Unit 17; SG Unit 12)
Figures with the same shape and size.

Convenient Number (URG Unit 6)
A number used in computation that is close enough to give a good estimate, but is also easy to compute mentally, e.g., 25 and 30 are convenient numbers for 27.

Coordinates (URG Unit 8; SG Unit 8)
An ordered pair of numbers that locates points on a flat surface by giving distances from a pair of coordinate axes. For example, if a point has coordinates (4, 5) it is 4 units from the vertical axis and 5 units from the horizontal axis.

Counting Back (URG Unit 2)
A strategy for subtracting in which students start from a larger number and then count down until the number is reached. For example, to solve $8 - 3$, begin with 8 and count down three, 7, 6, 5.

Counting Down (*See* counting back.)

Counting Up (URG Unit 2)
A strategy for subtraction in which the student starts at the lower number and counts on to the higher number. For example, to solve $8 - 5$, the student starts at 5 and counts up three numbers (6, 7, 8). So $8 - 5 = 3$.

Cube (SG Unit 18)
A three-dimensional shape with six congruent square faces.

Cubic Centimeter (cc)
(URG Unit 16; SG Unit 16)
The volume of a cube that is one centimeter long on each edge.

cubic centimeter

Cup (URG Unit 16)
A unit of volume equal to 8 fluid ounces, one-half pint.

D

Decimal Fraction (URG Unit 15)
A fraction written as a decimal. For example, 0.75 and 0.4 are decimal fractions and $\frac{75}{100}$ and $\frac{4}{10}$ are called common fractions. (*See also* fraction.)

Denominator (URG Unit 13)
The number below the line in a fraction. The denominator indicates the number of equal parts in which the unit whole is divided. For example, the 5 is the denominator in the fraction $\frac{2}{5}$. In this case the unit whole is divided into five equal parts.

Density (URG Unit 16)
The ratio of an object's mass to its volume.

Difference (URG Unit 2)
The answer to a subtraction problem.

Dissection (URG Unit 12 & Unit 17)
Cutting or decomposing a geometric shape into smaller shapes that cover it exactly.

Distributive Property of Multiplication over Addition (URG Unit 19)
For any three numbers *a, b,* and *c,* $a \times (b + c) = a \times b + a \times c$. The distributive property is the foundation for most methods of multidigit multiplication. For example, $9 \times (17) = 9 \times (10 + 7) = 9 \times 10 + 9 \times 7 = 90 + 63 = 153$.

E

Equal-Arm Balance
See two-pan balance.

Equilateral Triangle (URG Unit 7)
A triangle with all sides of equal length and all angles of equal measure.

Equivalent Fractions (SG Unit 17)
Fractions that have the same value, e.g., $\frac{2}{4} = \frac{1}{2}$.

Estimate (URG Unit 5 & Unit 6)
1. (verb) To find *about* how many.
2. (noun) An approximate number.

Extrapolation (URG Unit 7)
Using patterns in data to make predictions or to estimate values that lie beyond the range of values in the set of data.

F

Fact Family (URG Unit 11; SG Unit 11)
Related math facts, e.g., $3 \times 4 = 12$, $4 \times 3 = 12$, $12 \div 3 = 4$, $12 \div 4 = 3$.

Factor (URG Unit 11; SG Unit 11)
1. In a multiplication problem, the numbers that are multiplied together. In the problem $3 \times 4 = 12$, 3 and 4 are the factors.
2. Whole numbers that can be multiplied together to get a number. That is, numbers that divide a number evenly, e.g., 1, 2, 3, 4, 6, and 12 are all the factors of 12.

Fewest Pieces Rule (URG Unit 4 & Unit 6; SG Unit 4)
Using the least number of base-ten pieces to represent a number. (*See also* base-ten pieces.)

Flat (URG Unit 4; SG Unit 4)
A block that measures 1 cm × 10 cm × 10 cm. It is one of the base-ten pieces that is often used to represent 100. (*See also* base-ten pieces.)

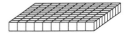

Flip (URG Unit 12)
A motion of the plane in which a figure is reflected over a line so that any point and its image are the same distance from the line.

Fraction (URG Unit 15)
A number that can be written as $\frac{a}{b}$ where a and b are whole numbers and b is not zero. For example, $\frac{1}{2}$, 0.5, and 2 are all fractions since 0.5 can be written as $\frac{5}{10}$ and 2 can be written as $\frac{2}{1}$.

Front-End Estimation (URG Unit 6)
Estimation by looking at the left-most digit.

G

Gallon (gal) (URG Unit 16)
A unit of volume equal to four quarts.

Gram
The basic unit used to measure mass.

H

Hexagon (SG Unit 12)
A six-sided polygon.

Horizontal Axis (SG Unit 1)
In a coordinate grid, the *x*-axis. The axis that extends from left to right.

I

Interpolation (URG Unit 7)
Making predictions or estimating values that lie between data points in a set of data.

J

K

Kilogram
1000 grams.

L

Likely Event (SG Unit 1)
An event that has a high probability of occurring.

Line of Symmetry (URG Unit 12)
A line is a line of symmetry for a plane figure if, when the figure is folded along this line, the two parts match exactly.

Line Symmetry (URG Unit 12; SG Unit 12)
A figure has line symmetry if it has at least one line of symmetry.

Liter (l) (URG Unit 16; SG Unit 16)
Metric unit used to measure volume. A liter is a little more than a quart.

M

Magic Square (URG Unit 2)
A square array of digits in which the sums of the rows, columns, and main diagonals are the same.

Making a Ten (URG Unit 2)
Strategies for addition and subtraction that make use of knowing the sums to ten. For example, knowing $6 + 4 = 10$ can be helpful in finding $10 - 6 = 4$ and $11 - 6 = 5$.

Mass (URG Unit 9 & Unit 16; SG Unit 9)
The amount of matter in an object.

Mean (URG Unit 5)
An average of a set of numbers that is found by adding the values of the data and dividing by the number of values.

Measurement Division (URG Unit 7)
Division as equal grouping. The total number of objects and the number of objects in each group are known. The number of groups is the unknown. For example, tulip bulbs come in packages of 8. If 216 bulbs are sold, how many packages are sold?

Measurement Error (URG Unit 9)
The unavoidable error that occurs due to the limitations inherent to any measurement instrument.

Median (URG Unit 5; DAB Unit 5)
For a set with an odd number of data arranged in order, it is the middle number. For an even number of data arranged in order, it is the number halfway between the two middle numbers.

Meniscus (URG Unit 16; SG Unit 16)
The curved surface formed when a liquid creeps up the side of a container (for example, a graduated cylinder).

Meter (m)
The standard unit of length measure in the metric system. One meter is approximately 39 inches.

Milliliter (ml) (URG Unit 16; SG Unit 16)
A measure of capacity in the metric system that is the volume of a cube that is one centimeter long on each edge.

Multiple (URG Unit 3 & Unit 11)
A number is a multiple of another number if it is evenly divisible by that number. For example, 12 is a multiple of 2 since 2 divides 12 evenly.

N

Numerator (URG Unit 13)
The number written above the line in a fraction. For example, the 2 is the numerator in the fraction $\frac{2}{5}$. (*See also* denominator.)

O

One-Dimensional Object (URG Unit 18; SG Unit 18)
An object is one-dimensional if it is made up of pieces of lines and curves.

Ordered Pairs (URG Unit 8)
A pair of numbers that gives the coordinates of a point on a grid in relation to the origin. The horizontal coordinate is given first; the vertical coordinate is given second. For example, the ordered pair (5, 3) tells us to move five units to the right of the origin and 3 units up.

Origin (URG Unit 8)
The point at which the *x*- and *y*-axes (horizontal and vertical axes) intersect on a coordinate plane. The origin is described by the ordered pair (0, 0) and serves as a reference point so that all the points on the plane can be located by ordered pairs.

P

Pack (URG Unit 4; SG Unit 4)
A cube that measures 10 cm on each edge. It is one of the base-ten pieces that is often used to represent 1000. (*See also* base-ten pieces.)

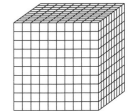

Palindrome (URG Unit 6)
A number, word, or phrase that reads the same forward and backward, e.g., 12321.

Parallel Lines (URG Unit 18)
Lines that are in the same direction. In the plane, parallel lines are lines that do not intersect.

Parallelogram (URG Unit 18)
A quadrilateral with two pairs of parallel sides.

Partitive Division (URG Unit 7)
Division as equal sharing. The total number of objects and the number of groups are known. The number of objects in each group is the unknown. For example, Frank has 144 marbles that he divides equally into 6 groups. How many marbles are in each group?

Pentagon (SG Unit 12)
A five-sided, five-angled polygon.

Perimeter (URG Unit 7; DAB Unit 7)
The distance around a two-dimensional shape.

Pint (URG Unit 16)
A unit of volume measure equal to 16 fluid ounces, i.e., two cups.

Polygon
A two-dimensional connected figure made of line segments in which each endpoint of every side meets with an endpoint of exactly one other side.

Population (URG Unit 1; SG Unit 1)
A collection of persons or things whose properties will be analyzed in a survey or experiment.

Prediction (SG Unit 1)
Using data to declare or foretell what is likely to occur.

Prime Number (URG Unit 11)
A number that has exactly two factors. For example, 7 has exactly two distinct factors, 1 and 7.

Prism
A three-dimensional figure that has two congruent faces, called bases, that are parallel to each other, and all other faces are parallelograms.

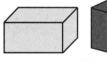

Prisms   Not a prism

Product (URG Unit 11; SG Unit 11; DAB Unit 11)
The answer to a multiplication problem. In the problem $3 \times 4 = 12$, 12 is the product.

Q

Quadrilateral (URG Unit 18)
A polygon with four sides.

Quart (URG Unit 16)
A unit of volume equal to 32 fluid ounces; one quarter of a gallon.

R

Recording Sheet (URG Unit 4)
A place value chart used for addition and subtraction problems.

Rectangular Prism (URG Unit 18; SG Unit 18)
A prism whose bases are rectangles. A right rectangular prism is a prism having all faces rectangles.

Regular (URG Unit 7; DAB Unit 7)
A polygon is regular if all sides are of equal length and all angles are equal.

Remainder (URG Unit 7)
Something that remains or is left after a division problem. The portion of the dividend that is not evenly divisible by the divisor, e.g., $16 \div 5 = 3$ with 1 as a remainder.

Right Angle (SG Unit 12)
An angle that measures 90°.

Rotation (turn) (URG Unit 12)
A transformation (motion) in which a figure is turned a specified angle and direction around a point.

Row (URG Unit 11)
In an array, the objects lined up horizontally.

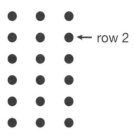
← row 2

Rubric (URG Unit 2)
A written guideline for assigning scores to student work, for the purpose of assessment.

S

Sample (URG Unit 1; SG Unit 1)
A part or subset of a population.

Skinny (URG Unit 4; SG Unit 4)
A block that measures 1 cm × 1 cm × 10 cm. It is one of the base-ten pieces that is often used to represent 10. (*See also* base-ten pieces.)

Square Centimeter (sq cm) (SG Unit 5)
The area of a square that is 1 cm long on each side.

Square Number (SG Unit 11)
A number that is the product of a whole number multiplied by itself. For example, 25 is a square number since $5 \times 5 = 25$. A square number can be represented by a square array with the same number of rows as columns. A square array for 25 has 5 rows of 5 objects in each row or 25 total objects.

Standard Masses
A set of objects with convenient masses, usually 1 g, 10 g, 100 g, etc.

Sum (URG Unit 2; SG Unit 2)
The answer to an addition problem.

Survey (URG Unit 14; SG Unit 14)
An investigation conducted by collecting data from a sample of a population and then analyzing it. Usually surveys are used to make predictions about the entire population.

T

Tangrams (SG Unit 12)
A type of geometric puzzle. A shape is given and it must be covered exactly with seven standard shapes called tans.

Thinking Addition (URG Unit 2)
A strategy for subtraction that uses a related addition problem. For example, $15 - 7 = 8$ because $8 + 7 = 15$.

Three-Dimensional (URG Unit 18; SG Unit 18)
Existing in three-dimensional space; having length, width, and depth.

TIMS Laboratory Method (URG Unit 1; SG Unit 1)
A method that students use to organize experiments and investigations. It involves four components: draw, collect, graph, and explore. It is a way to help students learn about the scientific method.

Turn (URG Unit 12)
(*See* rotation.)

Turn-Around Facts (URG Unit 2 & Unit 11 p. 37; SG Unit 11)
Addition facts that have the same addends but in a different order, e.g., $3 + 4 = 7$ and $4 + 3 = 7$. (*See also* commutative property of addition and commutative property of multiplication.)

Two-Dimensional (URG Unit 18; SG Unit 18)
Existing in the plane; having length and width.

Two-Pan Balance
A device for measuring the mass of an object by balancing the object against a number of standard masses (usually multiples of 1 unit, 10 units, and 100 units, etc.).

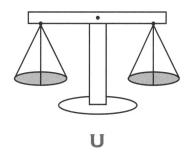

U

Unit (of measurement) (URG Unit 18)
A precisely fixed quantity used to measure. For example, centimeter, foot, kilogram, and quart are units of measurement.

Using a Ten (URG Unit 2)
1. A strategy for addition that uses partitions of the number 10. For example, one can find $8 + 6$ by thinking $8 + 6 = 8 + 2 + 4 = 10 + 4 = 14$.
2. A strategy for subtraction that uses facts that involve subtracting 10. For example, students can use $17 - 10 = 7$ to learn the "close fact" $17 - 9 = 8$.

Using Doubles (URG Unit 2)
Strategies for addition and subtraction that use knowing doubles. For example, one can find $7 + 8$ by thinking $7 + 8 = 7 + 7 + 1 = 14 + 1 = 15$. Knowing $7 + 7 = 14$ can be helpful in finding $14 - 7 = 7$ and $14 - 8 = 6$.

V

Value (URG Unit 1; SG Unit 1)
The possible outcomes of a variable. For example, red, green, and blue are possible values for the variable *color*. Two meters and 1.65 meters are possible values for the variable *length*.

Variable (URG Unit 1; SG Unit 1)
1. An attribute or quantity that changes or varies.
2. A symbol that can stand for a variable.

Vertex (URG Unit 12; SG Unit 12)
1. A point where the sides of a polygon meet.
2. A point where the edges of a three-dimensional object meet.

Vertical Axis (SG Unit 1)
In a coordinate grid, the *y*-axis. It is perpendicular to the horizontal axis.

Volume (URG Unit 16; SG Unit 16)
The measure of the amount of space occupied by an object.

Volume by Displacement (URG Unit 16)
A way of measuring volume of an object by measuring the amount of water (or some other fluid) it displaces.

W

Weight (URG Unit 9)
A measure of the pull of gravity on an object. One unit for measuring weight is the pound.

X

Y

Z